UNEXPECTED GUESTS AT GOD'S BANQUET

BRETT WEBB-MITCHELL

UNEXPECTED GUESTS AT GOD'S BANQUET

Welcoming People with Disabilities Into the Church

WIPF & STOCK · Eugene, Oregon

Wipf and Stock Publishers
199 W 8th Ave, Suite 3
Eugene, OR 97401

Unexpected Guests at God's Banquet
Welcoming People with Disabilities into the Church
By Webb-Mitchell, Brett
Copyright©1994 by Webb-Mitchell, Brett
Publication date: 2/23/2009
Previously published by Crossroad, 1994
Project# SP968

Contents

Acknowledgments

In 1989, I began work on this book, prior to the time I began publishing articles that would become *God Plays Piano, Too: The Spiritual Lives of Disabled Children*, which the Crossroad Publishing Company published in 1993. At first, it was a collection of chapters that attempted to apply theories of special education and music therapy to Christian religious education programs, assuming that Sunday schools were the primary model and avenue for educational ministry in the Church.

Much has changed since I began writing this book, including possible publishers and numerous revisions. Though at the time I couldn't understand why I had to wait so long to get this book finished and published, it appears that the waiting periods and rewrites may have been God's way of refining rough parts of this book. As a Presbyterian, I shall claim that God's providence was always at work, each step of the way, though rewriting is rarely a pleasant experience. God's Spirit propelled me on, and the book is complete . . . for now. And I am thankful that Mike Leach and the people of the Crossroad Publishing Company saw the importance of this book in the publishing world of theological ideas.

One of the most important chapters in writing this book is "Welcoming the Unexpected Guests to the Banquet." In Luke 14:15–24, Jesus' parable of the Great Banquet Feast gave me new insight not only into the nature of the Kingdom of God, but also, since the kingdom of God prefigures the church, into *why* people whom society has labeled "disabled" are inheritors of that Kingdom.

One of the implications of this chapter is that it has challenged my imagination to ponder what the Church *would* look, feel, hear, move, and act like if it understood itself as the Banquet Table of God's love on earth. Needless to say, the act of inviting, welcoming, and including people with a wide range of abilities and limitations into the church-as-God's-Banquet-Feast challenges many of the assumed programs and activities of the Church. For example, many of the educational practices of the Church are still being held captive by the public-school paradigm that the religious educator Dr. John Westerhoff remarked about years ago. Because the educational ministry of the Church is still based largely on the public-school paradigm, where logic, reasoning, and cognitive skills are primary modes of communication and learning, more churches are beginning to have religious special education programs. What is frightening about this trend is that many public schools are claiming that they no longer can afford special education programs, and some are even questioning the efficacy of these programs. There has begun a backlash against children with disabilities in the public schools. Is this what awaits children and adults with disabilities in the Church? While I have provided theory and practice for adapting programs and people with disabilities into the current world view of educational ministry of the Church, I am also presenting some challenging ideas about how we live out—or live in—the Church that accepts the analogy of being God's Banquet Feast on earth, with all of God's children. I am imagining, wondering, and sketching out what Christ intends the Church to be.

In writing this book, I owe a great deal of gratitude to my wife Pam, my daughter Adrianne and son Parker, as well as to my parents Elizabeth and Donald Mitchell and my in-laws Helen and Jim Webb. Writing books and trying out ideas all over the country in a variety of job opportunities places great strains on a family. Following one's dreams also has the potential of being a long, lonely venture, and I thank God that I have had the support of the family to remind me to take a break, go for a run, play in amusement parks, go to the movies, and enjoy an evening out at a fine restaurant.

This book is a culmination of my educational career as a music therapist and special educator, and of my time in theological institutions and pastoral opportunities in the Presbyterian Church (USA). Valley Community Presbyterian Church in Portland, Oregon, our "home" church, has a small missionary fund that I received money from more than once, to buy rhythm instruments for my educational ministry activities with children with disabilities in state hospitals, and to try out programs with people with disabilities in various parts of this country.

Writing a book is never a solo activity, and I want to thank members of the faculty, administration, students, and staff of Whitworth College in Spokane, Washington and Duke Divinity School in Durham, North Carolina, who listened to my ideas. I also thank the professional and paraprofessional staff and children who once worked and lived in a private, residential treatment center in Florida. Dr. Jim Paul, chairperson of the Special Education Department at the University of South Florida, read and reread, and listened again and again to the ideas that are in this book. Dr. John Westerhoff kept encouraging me to write the book while I was a doctoral student, and later, while I worked with him at Duke Divinity School. Dr. Stanley Hauerwas of Duke Divinity School has not only read many bits and pieces of this work, but his theological jousting made this book a better one.

Finally, I thank each and every group that I have presented portions of this book to, and every child and adult that I tried these ideas out on throughout the years. God has placed me in company with saints of the Church in all of these places. Their teaching style was concrete enough that even I understood the gist of what they were communicating. And their message was that God's Banquet Feast is awaiting us all. Soon enough, it will be time for all of us to take our place at this heavenly Banquet Feast that God has invited us to . . . before the food gets cold.

1

The Unexpected Guests:
The Betrayal of People
with Disabilities

I begin with some of the stories that I have collected from living, working, playing, and worshiping with people who have some kind of disabling condition in order to get to the point of this book: that many people, whom society has labeled and categorized as being disabled—those who are our unseen neighbors living next door—desire to come and be part of our congregations and parishes. The problem is that while a few have entered and been part of our churches, there are still many people outside, regardless of the wheelchair ramps and signing interpreters employed especially for "the disabled." They have either not been invited to come in, or even worse, have been disinvited. People with disabling conditions, including those who live life with a physical, developmental, behavioral, medical, emotional, hearing, or visual disability, are considered strange and different in a society that is primarily comfortable with those who look, sound, and act "normal"—whatever that is. Unfortunately, in this world, and even in many churches, "different" is still equated with "deviant."

To give the reader an idea of the problems that people with disabling conditions still face in churches, consider the following stories, told both by members of congregations who are learning how to invite people with disabilities into their churches, and by persons with disabilities who have been struggling to find the congregation or parish where they can worship God just as they are.

The Uninvited Guest

The first story concerns a church in the Boston, Massachusetts area and Jill,* a person who is coping with a mental illness.

Jill is a heavyset woman in her 40s, mother of four children and a wife for over 25 years. I met Jill through a friend, who happened to be her social worker, who shared Jill's anguish regarding the situation in this community.

Jill had recently moved back home to this suburban enclave after having spent the last 10 years in an institution because she could not control her mental illness. Part of her new therapy program included becoming involved in the local neighborhood's social life, such as activities at the YWCA and the church. Jill had heard about a church in the area that had a carpool system providing rides to the worship service on Sunday mornings. For over a year, Jill was faithful in her attendance at that church.

She enjoyed the worship service because she was able to sing and go to the coffee hour afterward, and because she "liked God." She had grown up in a Roman Catholic family, and recounted for me stories of singing solos in the local church's choir beginning when she was five years old, and she has enjoyed singing in the church ever since. She delighted in the coffee hour not only because of the food, but because she said this was her time "to get to know my neighbors."

Jill was dedicated to attending this church; it was part of her weekly schedule. It came as a shock to her when the rides to church stopped one Sunday. Thinking that someone had made a mistake, Jill continued to wait every Sunday for six weeks with no one coming to take her to church. Jill was dismayed and depressed. She felt cut off from the community of Christians that she had started to feel at home with after all these months; she had no idea what she had done to receive such treatment. Jill finally told her social worker what had transpired. It was then that the social worker asked me to talk with the pastor to find out what had occurred.

In talking with the pastor, I learned something about the history of this church and about a problem shared by many congregations regard-

---

*Throughout this entire book, all names will be changed for matters of confidentiality.

ing inclusion of persons with disabilities in a parish's life. First, the pastor was new to the church and had inherited this program from his predecessor, without any idea as to why it was being conducted. Many of those who were uncomfortable with Jill's presence asked him to stop this program, which he did, as he himself felt uncomfortable with her presence in the church.

What bothered this pastor was Jill's behavior. She sang too loud for many in the church; she answered the questions in the children's sermon before the children did. Jill told me later that she was unaware of the fact that these questions were only for children, as no one told her that during the worship service.

The pastor continued, telling me that Jill's body odor was offensive to many. Again, Jill explained that she was unaware of the problem, and she said she would leave the worship service when she knew she had to, which sometimes meant her leaving the pew during the pastor's sermon.

The last statement the pastor made was his doubt about Jill's awareness of what was happening in worship: "I don't know if Jill really understands the symbols of the worship service." When I asked him if he asked Jill if she understood the symbolism, the pastor said he never did get a chance to ask her.[1]

Architecture and Evangelism

The second story illustrates the congregation that wants to invite people with disabilities to come into the church; is ready to invest time, energy, and money; but has often forgotten to ask any person with a disabling condition to be part of the planning process. The setting is a large suburban nondenominational church in a large metropolitan area, asked by a family with a child who is physically impaired and in a wheelchair to see about making the physical structure of the building accessible to people with disabilities. The church leaders responded, calling together an ad-hoc committee composed of the senior pastor and associate pastor and some other men, including two architects and a builder. Somewhere, among the eight men I met was the treasurer, who reminded the committee of the expense of ramps and elevators. The person who was missing from this group was the little boy who was in the wheelchair, and his parents. These were the people who could best tell this committee what was needed to make the church accessible.

I was called in as a consultant to talk to this committee about the options available, given the physical structure of the church and the merchandise, like elevators and lifts, available for moving people in wheelchairs. We talked about elevators that accommodate only one wheelchair and one person to push the wheelchair. The pricetag was around $50,000, with another $100 per month for maintenance. We talked about scissor lifts between floors that would also cost thousands of dollars. A long ramp from the sanctuary to the education wing of the church would cost roughly $3,000, including knocking down some walls and moving doors to meet state building codes.

As we all walked around the church, we looked at what was already in place for persons in wheelchairs: There were four parking places in the front of the church for "handicapped parking," with another "handicapped parking" place by the education wing. However, the doors into the sanctuary and education–administration wing swung out toward the person rather than swinging into the building, which is easier for the person with a disabling condition.

We continued our walk around the church, trying to get an image of the maze of zigzagging ramps that would need to be installed outside. Going from the ground floor up to the second and third floor on a very gradual slope would mean a series of three or four long zigzagging ramps for each floor, and would cost thousands of dollars to construct.

Inside the building, the bathrooms were fairly accessible, though the handrails in the toilet area were not close enough to allow some people in wheelchairs to use the toilet independently. All the doorways within the building were just large enough to get an adult in a wheelchair through them, but not if the person were using her arms to maneuver.

In the sanctuary, we looked around the worship space. A visitor to the congregation who was in a wheelchair told the leaders that he was perfectly satisfied with the accommodations of the church, and he didn't minding sitting in the back of the church where the floor was level. Going toward the front of the sanctuary the floor sloped down to the pulpit, which was on a slightly raised stage. On either side of the pulpit were four steps that you had to go up in order to be seen by the congregation. There were more steps to get into the choir area.

When in the sanctuary, we began to talk among ourselves. One person asked the question: "Is this worth all the money that we are going to have to raise in order to make this building accessible? We only have one family with a child in a wheelchair; what happens when this particular family leaves? Then we won't have anyone else having to use it."

The senior pastor was interested in the evangelistic dimension of the enterprise: "How many people are there in the metropolitan area with disabling conditions? And how could we publicize the accessibility of this building, letting others know what we offer?" I suggested that once one group of people with disabling conditions knew of the church trying to become accessible to others, that news would spread along the grapevine among people in the disabilities community.

There was talk of providing helpful services for people with hearing impairments and visual impairments, and the possibility of helping people with mental retardation. I cautioned that it may be prudent to work on one disability concern at a time.

What was interesting about the discussion was that nowhere in our talk did the committee consider the opinion of the congregation or ask a person with a disability, or a group of people with disabilities, about what they should or could be doing to make the church sanctuary and the programs of the church accessible for all who wished to enter. They hadn't talked about it with the members of the church first, but were acting out of the need expressed by one family. There was no sense of congregational or grass-roots support and leadership for this project. Rather, the leaders were dictating what they could and would do for the people with disabilities. The voice of the person with a disabling condition was missing from the conversation.

The Teamwork of God and John

The third story is about John, whom I met while he was living in an institution for people with mental retardation, and about some of the strained relationships he has had with congregations where he lives.

John is in his mid-20s and has cerebral palsy, which limits the use of his legs and affects his speech as he slurs some words together. He also has dyslexia, a reading disability. Through accepting some of the limitations of his disabilities, John has learned to explore the broader use of his abilities and gifts. While he cannot read or write, John can memorize, talk, and listen to other people extremely well.

In one conversation with John, he stated clearly that he had always felt accepted by God, "or else God wouldn't have made me or put me here on earth." But John did not feel loved or accepted by his family or by the churches he tried in his life. Before John was born, his mother and father were living on welfare, working at odd jobs whenever possible. When John's mother was giving birth to John, his father took off, never to be seen again because he was overwhelmed by the burden of caring for another child on top of John's four older sisters. For years, John felt rejected by his mother because she had to give him up for adoption due to the home situation and to John's disabilities. It was not until he was nine years old that John first learned the reason he was put up for adoption at age three: His mother could not pay the bills for the corrective surgery or for the physical therapy that was sure to follow. The message John heard was, "No one wanted to adopt a crippled kid."

John was shuttled to three different foster homes and could not remember the first one. The second was what he called the "most abusive. They never hugged me. They put me on a chair and tied me down so I wouldn't fall off, or kept me in bed until sores would start to appear." At other times, without the use of a wheelchair, John was expected to crawl to the bathroom when he needed to; if he didn't get to the bathroom in time, one of the parents would put John in a cold bath for over an hour to clean him off, hoping that this would "encourage" him to get to the bathroom in time. The third family took better care of John, hugging and feeding him, taking care of his medical bills, and trying to help him walk. Because the couple in this home were in ill health, John, at six years of age, was placed in an institution for the mentally retarded.

Even though John doesn't appear mentally retarded, he believed that the educational services in the institution gave him this label due to his reading disability. In retrospect, John thinks it has been a good placement because he did get the physical therapy he needed, and was taught as well as possible. It was here that he learned to become more independent, more able to move his wheelchair around the campus, giving him some degree of autonomy in his life.

John has had varied experiences with faith communities in the area. He has attended both denominational and nondenominational faith communities. He remembers first taking God seriously when he was 13 years old. The reason he believes God first loved him is because he did not die with all the moves to different foster homes and institutions. His worst memory was a pastor of a small church who was sure that John's disability was caused by the devil. When they tried to exorcise the devil, John was sure they were going to exorcise him.

By contrast, John's acceptance of himself has resulted from his experience of being accepted and loved for who he is within a local congregation. Recently, a small group from a local congregation had come to talk with him "as if I really had a brain! Others who come here, oh, they just talk to us adults as if we were really little kids; drives me crazy." Feeling accepted for who he is by a congregation gives John freedom to explore other options for his future outside of the institution, in the larger community, as he continues to learn about himself, others, and God.

The emphasis here is on how John has moved from experiencing rejection by other people around him and his own poor self-image because of his disability, to acceptance of himself as he realized what his disability has already enabled him to accomplish. When John was asked what would happen if his disabilities were taken away, he replied he would lose his large arm muscles because he would not use his arms for the wheelchair as much:

> Let's put it this way: your ability, if you are close to God, comes with spirit. If you take away your ability, your spirit dies. If you take away my disability, I probably couldn't tell stories; but it's all teamwork, between God and myself. I've looked back on this disability. I probably would have been wilder without the disability. But the disability gives me strength. I ask God to continue to give me the energy to get around. And I do that pretty well with the wheelchair. The disability used to get me down because I used to be so slow. But people who think I can't do anything from this are always surprised when God and I get together. It's O.K. for you to prevent my getting hurt, but don't prevent God and John from doing things together.

John understands God's acceptance of him as grace. He understands that God is so patient with him, allowing him to go slow when he has to and accepting him when "I'm so damn stupid, as we all are." John holds to the knowledge that he is held securely by God's love in this world that is struggling to know him.[2]

Discovering Our Basic Assumptions of People with Disabilities

The third story has to do with the initial stages of inviting a child with disabling conditions into the life of the congregation. A new family had come to the church where I was working as a youth pastor, and they wanted to bring Steven with them when they came to worship. Steven was 12 years old, had spastic cerebral palsy that left him in a wheelchair for mobility, and was labeled severely mentally retarded as he was functioning with the mind of a one-year-old child.

There was a meeting arranged by the director of the Christian education program of this large suburban church. Invited to this meeting were Steven's mother and the lay leader of the Christian education program. I was invited because of my previous work with children with mental retardation. Steven's mother did an eloquent job giving us a picture of who Steven was and what his abilities and his limitations were in terms of his ability to function in the life of the congregation. Steven had been attending a special self-contained class for children with severe disabling conditions in the public school, and his mother brought along his Individualized Education Plan (I.E.P.) for us to look through after our meeting.

After Steven's mother talked with us about her son, an interesting collision of sorts occurred: The director of the Christian education program began to talk about the possibilities of moving Steven into the nursery school activities in the church during worship while I, at the same moment, began talking about moving pews and making adaptations in the worship service so that Steven could participate in worship! After we had been talking to Steven's mother at the same time, the director and I both stopped, looked at one another, and asked if what had happened had really happened. While both of us were wanting to bring Steven into the life of the congregation, we both had a vastly different vision for how he could participate. With some nervous laughter, we both spelled out our vision for Steven in the life of the congregation. We resolved the issue by deciding to try both options: Let Steven have some Sundays in the nursery school, and on some Sundays bring him to worship with the congregation.

"Look at Me as a Friend"

The final story is told by Joel, a 15-year-old "ski bum" who also has Down's syndrome. One summer, he came to share some time with his family at the Family Enrichment Conference at a Protestant Church retreat center. During this week, I worked with the families with children with disabilities, which included Joel's family. We tried something new at this retreat center: a "Best Buddy" program like other organizations working with children with developmental disabilities, pairing up the person with a disability with a non-disabled peer. At the time, Joel seemed to have had a good time. It wasn't until later that he shared with his mother what the week had been like for him:

1. Took too much of my time.
2. They did not have a golf course.
3. I got bored.
4. I didn't like the dance—too many people.
5. I didn't like being handicapped; I didn't like being called handicapped.

> I didn't like people telling me I needed a buddy. I liked Sam (his Best Buddy); he was fun to be with, *but* I don't like being called handicapped.
>
> To make it different next year, talk about what people can *do*, not what they can't do. Treat me like a friend, not like a person who can't do for themselves. Tell me what's fun to do with me. Have fun with me. Forget the handicapping condition. Look at me as a friend!

Unexpected Guests: The Church's Betrayal of People with Disabilities

What these stories reveal is the truth that there continues to exist an impregnable wall that separates the community of people with disabilities from our congregations and parishes. In Jill's story, the church was fearful of some of her behaviors. In the more evangelical congregation, some parishioners wanted to include people with disabilities but forgot to invite those with a disability to help in the very design of the program. As a person who had some motor difficulties, John, who *wanted* to be in the church, had a hard time convincing a congregation that he didn't need to be exorcised. In other cases, the large suburban church just didn't know what to do with Steven, the person with a disabling condition, once he was active in the life of the congregation. Finally, there was Joel, who said eloquently: "Forget the handicapping condition. Look at me as a friend!"

There are many questions that emerge from these truthful stories. One of the first and most important is: Who *is* the person with a disabling condition? Is the person to be understood or defined by his or her disability? This had been the response from many in society, which, in part, explains why many people talk about the "mentally retarded," "the disabled," "the deaf," or "the handicapped" as if this were a homogeneous crowd of people who walked, talked, and acted the same. The issue of labeling will be dealt with in this book, as what we have *called* people reveals how we treat individuals with disabling conditions.

Another question that comes from these stories is this: How do we put one's abilities and limitations, otherwise known as their disabling condition, into context? For example, John wanted to be treated as a friend, not as a charity project of the church. He wanted to be addressed in the following manner: "This is my friend, John." And if more information is needed, then you may add, "and John, by the way, needs a car big enough to get his wheelchair in the trunk." And Joel wanted to be known as a friend who liked to have fun, not as an object of pity for the "Best Buddy" program.

A final, key question that addresses the problem of the wall that divides the Church from people with disabilities: Why is Christ's living body on earth not only inhospitable but even hostile at times towards those with disabilities? Because the intent of many in our congregations and parishes is to make them just like us, and not for them to be just as they are. It is clear that many church members are struggling toward compassionately and effectively inviting, welcoming, and accepting the person with a disability into the congregation's life. However, if our congregations won't accept the person with a disability just as they are, as Christ calls us and accepts us, then it will fail to be a place where anyone who is different can grow in faith and knowledge of the Lord.

In sum, when the Church fails to invite and welcome people with disabilities, they have betrayed the very people with whom Christ closely identified during his life ministry. Those with disabilities are the same people whom Jesus was told by God not only to invite, but, in stronger language, to *compel* to come to the Great Banquet Feast of God's Kingdom (Luke 14:23). The founder of l'Arche, Jean Vanier, writes that Jesus revealed to us that he loves his Father, and is linked to him. At the same time Jesus is in love with each person, "and in a particular way with the most broken, the most suffering, and the most rejected . . . Jesus tells us that he is hidden in the face of the poor and those with disabilities, and that he is in fact the poor and disabled; to live with Jesus is to live with the poor (Matt. 25).[3]

One of the reasons that these uninvited guests are outside of the Church is because of an attitudinal barrier between those with disabilities and the "normal" people in congregations. The minister and disability advocate Harold Wilke talks about the prevalence of negative attitudes in religious communities toward people with disabilities. These attitudes are subtle yet entrenched against those that may be called "sickened-class" citizens.[4] This negative attitude is often expressed in the following ways. First, by outright rejection; people with disabilities are often put in the back of buses, churches, schools, and meetings, making them feel invalid. Second, by the overacceptance reaction, when avid church members swarm over people with disabilities "like a plague of locusts," proud of having a token "crip" in the crowd. Third, by sanctimonious exhortations, where people with disabilities receive almost verbal abuse; it is the failure of churches to invite, welcome, and accept another person who happens to have a disabling condition.

But the issue about attitudinal barriers is an abstract, theoretical explanation for a larger, deeper, and more insidious problem: It is our perception of people. How we perceive or envision and receive that person, seen through our distorted and biased lens of life, helps shape and inform our attitude toward others, determining in large part how we will treat and live with others who are not like us. It is our perception of others, learned in the culture we were raised in, that shapes out attitude toward all people, regardless of their ability or disability.

Perceptions of the Unexpected Guests

In his book *The Active Life* Parker Palmer discusses the power of illusion or perception that dictates how we see, relate to, and understand things to be real. We use illusions to get us through the day, whether the illusions help or hurt others around us. Some of the illusions explored are as follows:

> The illusion that violence solves problems, that both rich and poor deserve their own fate, that young people sent to die in wars fought to defend the rich are heroes rather than victims, that murderous drugs are the way beyond despair.[5]

Palmer writes that our illusions keep us in our place in society. As an example, he writes that if someone's child is murdered in a distant war for wealth, the military will award medals so parents can display them to keep from going mad.

Illusions, our perceptions of others, are strongly at work when it comes to the relationship between churches and people with disabilities. For those who are seemingly non-disabled, there is an image of people who have disabling conditions shaped, in part, by our families' reaction to them; the media's image and portrayal of people with disabling conditions, including television and print; by our experience in schools through integrated public school programs with other children who are disabled; and through other social-service agencies like the YWCA and YMCA, with their camps and after-school programs that include people with disabling conditions. By the time children are adults, having watched their parents' and siblings' reactions to and interactions with people who look different or sound different; who are in wheelchairs and who move and talk more slowly; who talk with their hands or walk with the aid of a cane or a dog, they have a perception, image, or, in some cases, an illusion of what people with disabling conditions can and cannot do—with emphasis on the latter.

Often the perception that non-disabled people have of those with a disabling condition is a mixture of much sympathy and little empathy, with an overwhelming sense of strangeness, as if the one who was disabled were from another planet. When I teach a class around the condition of mental retardation, I ask the class to take a moment and help me create a list of slang terms used to refer to the person with a disability. Moron, feeble-minded, retard or retarded, crip, super-crip, handicapped, gimpy, jerk, brain dead, fool, stupid, and microcephalic idiot are a few of the "favorites." When on the other side of the board I ask the students to name more favorable descriptions, they draw a blank. They say that they've heard few, if any, favorable descriptive terms about people with mental retardation, hearing impairments, or any other disabling condition.

Our perceptions of people with disabling conditions become the material that produces the brick and mortar of our attitudinal barriers between Christ's community of those who are non-disabled, and the community of people with disabling conditions. The perceptions have been enforced and reinforced throughout our lives. It is these unfavorable perceptions toward those with disabling conditions that many of those who are non-disabled bring to church. And these perceptions form our conscious reaction and our awkwardness around those who have a disabling condition.

For parents of children with disabling conditions, and for the person with a disability, the sense of rejection by friends or strangers on the street, or the possibility of rejection by other non-disabled people in a congregation, is most painful. For example, when I came before my church to be considered for ordination to the ministry, I met with the elders of my home church. I expressed to the group of elders my interest in helping build a connection or bridge of understanding between people with disabilities and the local church. During the question-and-answer period that followed my presentation, one of the elders asked if I had considered studying for a master's degree in social work rather than the parish ministry. Before I could open my mouth, a group of four elders spoke up for me. One of the elders had three children with microcephalus, a condition where the brain does not grow large enough, stunting the growth of the brain and resulting in mental retardation. Another elder had a young son who had just been diagnosed as having schizophrenia; the other two elders said that they each had a child who living in a state institution for children with mental retardation, which was a complete surprise to the other twenty members of the session of the church, who had no idea that there was such a need in the congregation. But the parents felt awkward and ashamed of having children with disabilities, fearing other people's perceptions of and reactions towards those with a disabling condition.

In the following section, there will be a brief survey of how these perceptual impressions have clouded and distorted the way many parishioners envision those who have different abilities and limitations. The list is by no means exhaustive, but rather typical of what is shared within and among many members in the Christian community when discussing the place and presence of people with disabilities in Christ's body.

Exploring Societal Images
of People with Disabilities

The "Thing" Is Contagious

The "thing" in this description is a person, a human being who, along with other abilities and limitations, has a disabling condition.

. ..ll-ulsabled people have pointed fingers and kept away from touching those with a disabling condition for fear that they too could come down with a disability. Even parents tell children not to touch, hug, or get too close to a person with a disability, from the fear that the condition may be contagious. Unlike the flu, a cold, and certain viruses, disabling conditions, such as a physical impairment or a hearing or visual problem, or mental retardation or mental illness, are not contagious. Yet some people even unconsciously avoid a person with a disabling condition, walking far away, even to the other side of the road if they see someone coming toward them in a wheelchair, on crutches, or using a cane or a seeing-eye dog.

A Symbol of Sin

Even though Jesus makes it clear to his disciples that the man who is blind from birth is not blind due to his own sin or the sin of his parents (John 9:1–12) there is still a non-disabled person somewhere in a congregation who is able to convince others that a disabling condition is the practical manifestation of an unknown sin. Like the friends of Job in the Hebrew Scriptures, they gather around either the family members or the person with a disabling condition, asking the person to remember exactly what it was that they did that offended God so much that they had a child with a disabling condition.

Parents of children with disabling conditions have, in many situations, borne the brunt of this strange interpretation of Scripture. In the book *There's A Difference in the Family*,[6] the special educator Helen Featherstone writes about her pain on giving birth to a child with a disabling condition and her lingering resentment toward God:

> If a healthy child is a perfect miracle of God, who created the imperfect child? Why would God create imperfection? Especially in a child? Especially in our child.[7]

Some psychologists suggest that there is a period of mourning and grief that many parents have to go through as the perception of their child as the "Gerber baby" dies and they learn to accept their baby with a disabling condition.[8] Featherstone and other parents of children with disabilities talk about the worry of a God of retribution who is now punishing them for some known or unknown sin with the deformation of their children. This is a perception of God as a cruel and tyrannical master who delights, in a strange, sadistic fashion, in creating these symbols of sin.

The Holy Innocents

In medieval Europe, people with mental retardation were often perceived as "Holy Innocents" and "children of God," being well received by all religious sects. As one of Scotland's Doric poets wrote:

> Nor is there ane amang ye but the best
> Wi' him wad share;
> Ye mauna skaith the feckless!
> They're God's peculiar care.[9]

This belief that people with mental retardation or other disabling conditions may be closer to God or more innocent than others who are non-disabled continues to this day. Even the famous astronomer Tycho Brahe (1546–1601), had a "colleague" who was mentally retarded. He kept a little person, Zep, who was "an imbecile to whose mutterings the great astronomer listened as a divine revelation."[10]

Many considered people with mental retardation as God's innocents, not in need of either justification or sanctification, and therefore they were neither baptized nor included in the Lord's Supper for they were not quite considered human and were believed to fall short of God's glory.

Images of a Lesser God

In the book *God in Creation,* the theologian Jurgen Moltmann argues that even when human beings sin, while it may pervert human beings' relationship to God, it does not pervert God's relationship to human beings. That relationship was resolved upon by God, and was created by God, and therefore cannot be withdrawn except by God. God's presence is in the lives of human beings as we are "un-deprivably and inescapably God's image."[11] Because of the relationship of God with men and women, the "handicapped person is also God's image in the fullest sense of the word; the image is in no way a diminished one." Moltmann, in a footnote, writes that his theological stance is contrary to the perception of the theologian Helmut Thielicke, who calls a person who is severely mentally retarded an "off-duty image of God."[12]

This concept of a God who is either off-duty or perhaps asleep at times in creation was upheld in the play and movie *Children of a Lesser God*. It focuses on the complex web of life that occurs in a school for students with hearing impairments. The students with hearing impairments are the children who, because of their disabling condition, reflect a lesser God, or an imperfect God in an imperfect world. People with disabling conditions become, in some way, a symbol of a God who is neither omnipresent nor omniscient. They become symbols of a God who is limited in creation, who stands by on the sidelines of life, hoping and cheering for the team to win but unable to step in and save the day.

Finally, there is this conversation between a mother and her physically impaired daughter:

> From the time Michelle was old enough to question her birth defects, we have always answered, "You were born this way. God made you." And the answer was sufficient.
>
> But recently she asked, "Why did God make me with no feet and two fingers?"
>
> "We don't always know why God does things, Michelle."
>
> "Well, I wish I was like everyone else. Anyway, God is not like this. How would He like it?"[13]

Suffering Personified

In his book *Suffering Presence* the Christian ethicist Stanley Hauerwas asks the question: Do those with mental retardation understand that they are mentally retarded? Surely they suffer from the same physical ailments anyone else may have, and they also die. But does their physical situation brought on by their disabling condition itself make people who are mentally retarded suffer? The answer is no.[14]

Then why is it that some social service professionals and others think that people with mental retardation are suffering? Hauerwas suggests that it may be related to the non-disabled community projecting how they would feel, given their current standard of life, if they were suddenly impaired. I have heard many times in the community of people who are non-disabled: "If I were mentally retarded, I know I would be hurting." This may be true since we are projecting our lives into what we assume is the life of another person; we are taking our perceptions, our illusions of what it would be like if our abilities were suddenly our limitations, and deciding that it would be too painful to bear. Therefore, if we are hurting and suffering from this abstract exercise of projection, surely the person with mental retardation is suffering.

But this is contrary to my experience with people who are mentally retarded. When visiting a l'Arche community near my home in Spokane, I asked some of the people I know who are mentally retarded if they hurt or suffer from anything in life. One young man with mental retardation said that he hurt himself in the workshop when a hammer accidentally fell on his foot; another person said he was tired of walking to and fro from his home to the l'Arche workshop down the street. One young woman shyly told me she was exhausted from washing the dishes after dinner. But no one said they were hurting or suffering from the condition of mental retardation.

Perceptions of Those with Disabilities

There are also the perceptions that the community of people with disabilities have toward those in power in largely non-disabled congregations and parishes:

Jesus the Crutch

Not all people with disabilities are necessarily eager or anxiously waiting for congregations to open their doors and invite them into worship. Some people with a disabling condition see Jesus and God as one more crutch in life that they would rather do without. Being a Christian or a Jew is not necessarily something respected among others in some disabilities communities. It is seen as weakness, as giving in to some parental or paternalistic forces in society. Anyone who needs God or needs Jesus may be considered weak and really feeble in the eyes of the disability community.

An Impregnable Fortress Is Our Church

In some disabilities communities, there is anger at congregations for being so inaccessible architecturally and attitudinally. The logic working here is that if the Church is mindful of the needs of those with disabilities, then at least their buildings would show their welcome. Instead, even though some churches are unable to afford the placement of ramps and elevators, they are perceived as being closed off from the disabilities community, if not openly hostile and emotionally cold toward its members. While some disabilities communities are working toward freedom and independence, arguing for the rights of those who are disabled, believing in God in Christ may be seen as a sign of submissive surrender, not of freedom and liberation. As I was told by a member of "People First," a national self-advocacy group of people with mental retardation, the churches and synagogues are the oppressors in need of liberation by the oppressed who are disabled. People with disabilities are eager to get on with life rather than trying to open doors of churches where there is no wheelchair ramp.

Playing Disabled

The problem in integrating people with disabilities in congregations is one of images. The non-disabled community in many of our congregations has nurtured their image of people with disabilities as the "suffering ones" and have found comfort in the illusion of the person with a disability being less than human. Many who are non-disabled feel sorry for the disabling condition, feeling guilty that they themselves do not have a disability. To assuage their guilt, many who are non-disabled are willing to do all kinds of good works to relieve themselves of the pain of guilt and the eternal suffering of the disabled.

Sensing this sorrow and guilt, some people with disabilities act more disabled than they really are, taking advantage of the unassuming non-disabled person and refusing to do on their own things they are capable of. For example, until recently, a young man who has autistic behaviors never cleaned himself after going to the bathroom at home. However, the schoolteacher always insisted that he take care of himself when going to the bathroom at school. Why didn't the son take care of himself in the home? George, the young man with autism, said: "Because my mother thinks I'm autistic and can't do anything."

Some of those who are non-disabled, both clergypeople and laity in congregations, nurture these illusions, these stereotypical images, in hopes of keeping those who are disabled in their places. Some people with disabilities also nurture their illusions and stereotypes about the Church. The by-product of these misperceptions and images are stereotypes and the building of walls and barriers that have been strongly reinforced throughout time, in all cultures, and among all Christian communities. They have withstood the test of time and have yet to be truly torn down.

An Invitation to the Banquet

The goal of this book is to call forth and challenge the collective imagination of congregations and parishes, including both members who are non-disabled and those with disabilities, to be and become more like Christ's community on earth by inviting, welcoming, and accepting those people whom Christ initially invited but who we have left outside. It is by the power of the Holy Spirit that Christ calls all of us, regardless of our abilities and limitations, toward the Kingdom of God.

In inviting and welcoming people with disabilities, the Church acts not out of charity only but from a desire to receive one another as a source of life and communion. Those with disabilities are invited by Christ not to be liberated, but for the Church to be liberated by them; not to heal their wounds, but to be healed by them; and not to evangelize them, but to be evangelized, for they lead us deeper into our faith in Jesus Christ.[15]

This book will provide both the theological rationale as well as the pragmatic steps that should be considered as congregations move toward the active integration of vital members with a unique set of unexplored abilities and real tangible limitations. Not only *how, what* and *when*, but the theological and biblical roots for *why* people with disabling conditions should be part of congregational life will be discussed. There will be a mixture of stories, theological reflections, practical suggestions, and new questions concerning the place and presence of people with disabilities in congregations.

This book assumes that the higher calling of Christian religious education is to lead people to the Kingdom of God,[16] as preached and lived by Jesus Christ.[17] The very nature of the Church is guided by the shared vision that the members have of the Kingdom of God. Jesus wisely understood that if God's message of love was to be clearly understood by the masses, including his disciples, then he would have to tell them parables or short stories (Mark 4:11). For example, the guiding parable for the Kingdom of God image in this book is the parable of the Great Banquet (Luke 14:15–24, NIV).

Jesus begins the story by telling the listeners that "someone gave a great dinner and invited many. At the time for the dinner he sent his slave to say to those who had been invited, 'Come; for everything is ready now.'" In the parable, the three invited guests turned down God, the Host's, invitation. Jesus, the servant in the parable, was sent out into the streets and lanes of the town to bring in the poor, "the crippled, the blind, and the lame" (verse 21). The people who were poor, those who were disabled, suddenly and unexpectedly became the invited guests to God's banquet of love, the Kingdom of God. The message for the Church today: If the Church is to be like the Kingdom of God, then it too must invite, welcome, and accept the presence of those who are considered poor, "the crippled, the blind, and the lame" in our world today.

The method of working with congregations and parishes in being like the Great Banquet is through Christian religious education. Christian religious education is not understood in this book to be exclusively happening in a Sunday school class, a youth program, an adult Bible study, or preschool activities. Instead, Christian religious education is to be understood as all-inclusive in nature: *Everything* that happens in the church is Christian religious education, from worship on Sunday morning to fellowship hour and potlucks. Churches do not just have a religious education staff, but the congregations and parishes as a whole are the Christian religious educators.[18] The Church *is* Christian education.

Chapter 2 will focus on what special educators and psychologists consider a "disabling condition" or a "disability." It will focus on the labels and categories used for describing certain disabling conditions. But there will also be the exploration of the fragility of naming a condition, and how powerfully dangerous labeling can be in how a person with a disabling condition perceives him or herself, but also in how the larger community experiences the other who is disabled.

Chapter 3 is a brief historical and theological overview of the Jewish and Christian story in terms of the place of people with disabilities in the life of the community. Both the Old Testament and the New Testament reveal how people with disabling conditions were perceived by not only the human community, but also, more importantly, by God.

However, the story does not end there. Chapter 3 will also briefly explore how the church has sometimes welcomed and at other times violently rejected those people with disabling conditions.

In Chapter 4 there is a story of the Great Banquet Feast, the central thematic image for the Kingdom of God in this book. According to the Gospel of St. Luke, Jesus tells the Pharisees and disciples gathered together for dinner about a banquet table with some unexpected guests: Neither the guests themselves nor the people hearing the story for the first time expected to be there. The only one who may have truly understood this story is the God of the Messianic banquet, the Lord and Master of the Banquet feast. We will explore how this story can be a model for helping congregations and parishes alike to work toward discovering this model gathering of all who wish to come. Most importantly, we'll examine the role and function of people with disabling conditions in the life of Christian communities. Again, the goal is toward the integration and inclusion of people with disabling conditions in the life of the parishes and congregations.

In Chapter 5, there will be examples of how congregations can begin the movement toward inviting, then welcoming, and finally learning to accept people with disabling conditions into the life of the congregation.

In Chapter 6, we will look at ways of adapting existing Christian religious education curriculum, especially children's programs and worship activities, so that people with various disabling conditions can take an active part in a church's worship.

In Chapter 7, there is an exploration of Christian religious education programs for and with people with disabilities and those who are non-disabled, based upon the intentional act of learning and practicing the "peculiar" gestures of Christ's people.

In Chapter 8, after exploring the theological and biblical basis for including all those who wish to enter our congregations' life, and with better knowledge of the abilities and limitations some people face due to their disabling condition, we will look at some stories of churches that are celebrating life as more integrated congregations, and what the Church's example may mean for other communities that include people with disabling conditions.

In conclusion, our reaching out to one another is full of hope and doubt, joy and heartache, pleasure and pain, as both communities will be doing something new. Both the non-disabled community of the church and the community of those with disabilities will be pushed out of what is comfortable as they tear down ancient illusions and antiquated perceptions that maintain an unhealthy and unholy status quo. Like the world around us, congregations and parishes live in opposition, or, as historian Michel Jeanneret contends, in a divided world:

> A world in which physical and mental pleasures are compartment-alized and ordered into a hierarchy: they either conflict with each other or are mutually exclusive . . . However, the banquet is the one thing that overcomes this division and allows for the reconcili-ation of opposites . . . [In banquets] the combination of words and food in a convivial scene gives rise to a special moment when thought and the senses enhance rather than just tolerate each other . . . At table we rediscover, in the imagination, elements of origi-nal happiness and unity.[19]

Inviting and welcoming those with disabilities, who have lived out-side the confines of our churches, will help undo the pain of betrayal that many have felt for many years. With the inclusion of those with disabilities, the Church as God's Great Banquet will become a most "convivial scene" as we all rediscover, in the imagination of our collec-tive hearts, God's loving presence in our very midst.

2

• • •

What Shall We Call "Them"? The Issue of Labels and Categories

One of the most difficult and complex issues when confronted by people with disabilities is the automatic "we–they" barrier. Even in writing this book, identifying the issue of Christian religious education and ministry with people with disabling conditions strongly suggests to the reader that this is a book that will be primarily on and about issues involving *only* people with disabling conditions in congregational life. However, there is much more in this book that is pertinent to all people, regardless of their abilities or limitations, because it is first and foremost a book about human beings created in the image of God. The only difference is that the specific limitations some people have are manifested either mentally, emotionally, physiologically, or physically. These manifestations have been rigorously labeled and categorized by the surrounding, so-called normative culture as being an "impairment" or a "handicap."[20]

The issue of labeling and categorizing a disabling condition is important for the people in Christian communities to understand because we are strongly influenced by the norms used by professionals in society when working with people who are disabled. Congregations and parishes have, in large part, accepted the labels and categories the surrounding culture uses for determining who a person with a disability is, and how to address him or her. For example, on the national level almost each denomination has a special office for people with disabilities. Sometimes, congregations try to use a different language, like "differently abled," "handicapable," or "physically challenged," but this further confuses rather than clarifies the issue: It still marks certain people as different because of what they *cannot* do.

This idea of a mark that people with disabling conditions wear due to their limitations is addressed by the sociologist Erving Goffman. In his book *Stigma*, he writes that the term "stigma" originally was used by the ancient Greeks to refer to a bodily sign that is created to designate something abnormal and bad about the moral status of the one marked. These signs were either cut or burned into a person's body, showing all that the person was a slave, a criminal, or a traitor to the state.[21]

The ancient Greeks' world view continues to influence how we envision or perceive a person who may have a physically visible disability that we often think of as a stigma, a tragic mark. The child with Down's syndrome who is mentally retarded, with his round head and narrow eyes and his small stature, looks like someone who is different than the "rest of us." The young teenager who lost his sight due to a car accident uses a white cane when walking down the crowded street; the adult with cerebral palsy, whose spasms are sometimes uncontrollable, physically shakes as she wheels herself down a hall in a wheelchair; the young man with the condition of dwarfism is exceptionally small in stature.

We have all seen what happens when one with these disabling conditions comes down the street. We give them a wide berth, stay out of their way, try not to look too hard when it seems like a natural inclination to stare at that which is different than what society has deemed normal. We don't stare at the person who wears glasses or a hearing aid because these aids are more socially acceptable. But give us a person with a more obvious physical disability and we react as if they had a stigma that labeled them "different," and therefore possibly physically or morally dangerous.

The book, *Images Of Ourselves*, contains stories told by women with disabilities about their experiences of having a disabling condition. Consider Sue's moving autobiography. This is a passionate story told by a woman with multiple sclerosis who writes eloquently about her feeling regarding becoming a member of "THE DISABLED; the beginning of the frightening descent into the world of the social minority":

The "sick role" is society's niche for THE DISABLED. You must behave as "the sick" at all times but never complain about it. You must allow your person to have good works vented upon it, it makes THEM feel better, accept with a gracious smile the fuss, offers of "help" you don't need. It puts you in the "sick role"—the good feel good, everyone is happy. "They are just trying to help"—but whom they are actually helping is supposition in need of analysis that these good souls would never attempt.[22]

Who are "us?" Who are the normal people in our world whom others are judged by? What are the defining characteristics of what is considered "normal" and "abnormal?" The special educator Nicholas Hobbs wrote the following characteristics for identifying what is normal, good, and acceptable in America:

1) to be rational, 2) to be efficient in the use of one's time and energy, 3) to control distracting impulses and to delay gratification in the service of productivity, 4) to value work over play, 5) to be thrifty, 6) to be economically and socially successful and ambitious, 7) to be independent and self-reliant, 8) to be physically whole, healthy, and attractive, 9) to be white, 10) to be native born, 11) to be Protestant, 12) to be intellectually superior, 13) to inhibit aggressive and sexual behaviors except in specially defined situations, and 14) to be fluent in American English.[23]

This is the secret normative standard by which many in society, including the Church, determine who is able bodied and who is disabled, who is "us" and who is "them."

In this chapter, we will look at the rational arguments for why there is labeling and categorizing of disabling conditions, as well as at criticism of the practice. This is to remind the reader that labeling and categorizing is, at best, imperfect and changing. Yet this issue is a part of the reality that Christian religious educators and lay leaders in churches need to understand as we work toward the goal of including children and adults with disabling conditions in the lives of parishes and congregations.

Following this discussion will be descriptions of many disabling conditions people may have who come to our congregations and parishes. In closing, there is a discussion of the importance of acknowledging that we are all human, regardless of what wonders we perform or what blunders we make in the world in the presence of God.

The "Whys" and "Why Nots" of Labels and Categories

In the 1970s, there was a famous study on the classification of exceptional children, conducted by Nicholas Hobbs, which resulted in the book, *The Futures of Children*.[24] In short, the study was to increase the general public's awareness of the serious problems of labeling and categorizing with the hopes of providing a general outline for future generations of professionals involved in and responsible for the "well-being of exceptional children." This list included "educators, psychologists, physicians, lawyers, social workers." To this list I will add religious educators as well, Christian and Jewish alike.

Hobbs correctly states the seriousness of the task of labeling and categorizing as it can truly change what happens in the life of a child or an adult when one has been labeled as being "disabled." It can make it possible for important early intervention services and programs to be delivered and administered to a child with a disabling condition, providing the child new hopes and opportunities. However, an inappropriate label applied to a child can have such serious effects that it will damage not only the life of this person, diminishing self-esteem and even humanity, but it will also damage the person's family, friends, and supporting community.[25]

From his work in this study on classification with Hobbs, the special educator James Gallagher wrote an article considering the "sacred and the profane" uses of labels and categories.[26] Under the theme of the "sacred" uses of labels and categories he made some important points as to why they are needed:

First, labels and categories serve the important role of naming a condition that seems abnormal as soon as possible. According to Gallagher, labels begin the process of a "classification, diagnosis and treatment sequence peculiarly designed to counteract certain identifiable negative conditions." Common sense dictates that the earlier a disabling condition can be identified, the sooner attention can be focused on either curing it or preventing it from worsening.

Second, labels and categories can often open up important doors of opportunity in providing the necessary services or treatments. This will enable the person who is disabled to more fully adapt to the surrounding culture to the point of being in the "least restrictive environment."

Given our knowledge of some basic characteristics that keep occurring as a result of some disabling conditions, labels and categories may provide a shortcut method for understanding certain dynamics of specific disabilities. For example, knowing how much a person who has a hearing impairment or has residual hearing can hear will help the speech and hearing experts to know whether or not to use hearing aids along with other methods of communication. Knowledge of certain physiological conditions associated with Down's Syndrome can direct physicians to check the hearts of children with this condition, as many have heart problems.

Third, labels and categories also become helpful when dealing with funding sources, whether from federal and state governmental sources or from private foundations and religious organizations. They give an idea about what programs they are funding and who would be receiving their money. The use of labels and categories are a shorthand way of placing people together rather than drawing out the narrative of each person and each program that would be receiving money. In a way, knowledge of what a person with "cerebral palsy" or a "learning disability" might be like speeds the process of writing legislation or applying for funds.

The Dangers of Labeling

Both Hobbs and Gallagher also list some important "BEWARE" signs concerning the "profane uses" of labeling and categorization. As Hobbs writes, labels and categories can be used in ways that shut tightly the doors of opportunity, becoming a way for some people in society to control and regulate what a person with a disabling condition can, and more often cannot, do:

> "They [labels and categories] degrade people . . . denying them access to opportunity, to exclude "undesirables" whose presence in some way offends, disturbs familiar custom, or demands extraordinary effort."[27]

The act of labeling and categorizing someone, whether it is written or spoken, has powerful social implications. The family therapist Salvador

Minuchin wrote that the act of labeling is a social phenomenon. As a social phenomenon, the speaker and the one being spoken to are united by their common understanding, their shared ideology, that helps them, in part, know what a label means. He uses the example of the word "Jude" which determined one's form of death, as would a yellow star of David on a coat during World War Two.[28] Labeling someone has powerful implications in our society, revealing society's prevailing ideology.

Other possible dangers with labels are as follows:

First, the danger that labeling may be a "means for tranquilizing professionals by applying labels to children without following through with subsequent differentiated programs of treatment."[29] One of the dangers of classification is that, for some, the goal is to classify a child's condition—period, with little regard for the next step after diagnosis.

Many times, in professions working with people who are disabled, the goal is to identify the disabling condition. Period. The follow-up is to be done by, say a speech therapist or a psychologist, depending on the condition. However, I have read many records where a person's condition was listed, but no plans were outlined for dealing with the condition.

Second, sometimes labels have been used to preserve a "social hierarchy by using labels to keep minority-group children from opportunities and to force them to remain at the bottom of the social ladder."[30] For example, in a study of children in special education programs in California, researchers found that there was an oversupply of Spanish-surname children who could not speak English yet were in special education programs based on their performance on a standard American IQ test.[31]

Third, all labels are time bound, established, and written for and by people who live and exist in a certain cultural context. For example, up to the early 1960s, there was not a significant number of children in the United States who had a "learning disability," so that this condition was not listed or defined by Congress in Public Law 88-164, the Mental Retardation Facilities and Community Mental Health Centers Construction Act of 1963. But in 1974–1975, after the condition had been legislated as a disabling condition in 1968, about 2 million children were labeled as having a learning disability (compared to 1.5 million who were listed as mentally retarded).[32] In other words, there wasn't a child with a learning disability in the world until the "disabling condition" had been legislated by the U.S. Congress in the 1960s.

Another example of the frailty of these labels can be found when looking at the label "mental retardation." In the medieval ages, people with mental retardation were known as "simple idiots" or "morons." During the 19th century, people with mental retardation in the United States were called "mentally deficient." In the late 19th and early 20th centuries, they were seen as the "feeble minded," and many institutions for people with mental retardation were called "colony for the feeble minded." In the latter part of the 20th century we have addressed people with this condition as having a developmental disability, such as "mental retardation."[33]

There is also the story of the "Six-Hour Retarded Child." These children are labeled as being mentally retarded and put into six hours of special education classes because of their I.Q. score. But outside of the classes, these children are quite bright, functioning "quite normally in their home and community environments."[34]

As for the importance of cultural context and how social systems can confuse laypeople with labels, categories, and abbreviations for disabling conditions, consider the following example. In America, the disabling condition "learning disability" is often abbreviated as "L.D." However, in England, a person who, in America, is categorized as being mentally retarded is referred to as a person with "L.D.," which means a "learning *difficulty.*"

Fourth, the focus is often on the deficit and the limitation, rather than on a child's abilities, or what the child can *do,* let alone who the child *is.* Many of the assessment tests created and developed by professionals focus largely on discovering what a child or an adult with a disability *cannot* do. Numbers are given to show what a person's "intelligence quotient" is, as if intelligence could be "quantified." I.Q. scores, like other standardized test scores, are a combination of some very high and very low scores, with the low scores perhaps showing the reader weak areas in a student's academic life.

Unfortunately, this number is often generalized to other areas of life, taken to demonstrate all that the person cannot do rather than giving both stories of what a person may not be able to do in one setting and may be able to do in another. Many of these tests, like the Stanford-Binet I.Q. test and the Graduate Record Examination, were created to guide professionals in making choices about letting people into programs, not to place these people in boxes that limit their future.

The scores from these standardized tests were meant to be a practical device, a rough guide for identifying people with mental retardation or learning disabilities who need help, not to serve as a ranking for normal children. The science historian Steven Jay Gould wrote that these tests are not designed to define anything innate or the potential a person has in a yet unexplored area of intelligence.[35]

Fifth, who has the power to define what is normal and abnormal in society? According to a recent article in *U.S. News and World Report*, it is clear that the classification system used by the American Psychiatric Association has much of the power. When their first Diagnostic and Statistical manual of Mental Disorders (DSM) came out in 1952, there were only 106 disorders. In the latest version there are 292 possible diagnoses, from "Schizophrenia" to a new disorder, "Hypoactive Sexual Desire Disorder." There is fear that the power of naming a disorder has gotten out of hand, challenging what once were considered "individual choice, habit, eccentricity, or lifestyle" choices.[36]

In conclusion, the process of labeling and categorizing is an imperfect and subjective science, based on human judgment in a certain time, place, and cultural context. Because the process of labeling and categorizing is bound by human judgment, labels and categories merely reflect our present incomplete understanding of disabling conditions that have been identified among human beings.

Overall, when using and referring to the many conditions, it is important to remember that we are often using inaccurate, time-bound, culture-bound, context-dependent terms that are bound to change, even during the time that this book is published. Labels and categories are social phenomenon, human constructions, all apt to change throughout history. There is nothing absolute about any of them.

One of the best ways to look at or approach the issue of labels and categories may be found in the book *Pathways to Madness* by the psychologist and anthropologist Jules Henry, which concerns disturbed families.[37] Human language is ambiguous at best because everything is so poorly defined and because different theorists and writers use the same words with different meanings. The language that we use in labels and categories are mere pointers, signs on life's journey, that are not there to control the destiny of people. Rather, the signs say that, while another person is human, there is nonetheless something unique about this or that person and how he or she interacts with the world, the behavior they display, or the limitations and abilities that they portray.

One other cautionary note: All of these labels are determined by the norms of the society congregations and parishes are set in. But what many churches need to remember is that they see themselves as a cultural context unique unto itself. The Church needs to think about whether or not a person whose limitations are defined by the professionals in society would be labeled as "disabled" in the context of the Christian community that lives by a different set of norms and serves a particular God.

What Shall We Call "Them"?

Each field or discipline involved in caring for and being with people with disabling conditions has their own descriptions and definitions. In this section, we will explore the given standard definition for the disabling condition used in special education, followed by a more descriptive explanation of the condition.

Mental Retardation

"Mental retardation" is a term that has been popular for a long time on the playgrounds and in the public schools, and churches, of America. If you really wanted to get someone angry as a child, then you just called that person a "tard" or "retard." We have made fun of those who are slow at completing a task, saying, "What are you, retarded?" Other "favorite" expressions are "moron," "idiot," perhaps "mentally deficient," or maybe "feeble-minded." The sad truth is that throughout history we have called people with this disabling condition such names.

Some people with mental retardation have scared others because of the way they look and myths of animal-like behavior that may be tied back into the classic studies and examples of children, such as the boy who may have been mentally retarded, *The Wild Boy of Aveyron*, by Jean-Marc-Gaspard Itard in the late 18th or early 19th century.[38] In this study, the French physician tried to educate a young boy who displayed wild, animal-like behavior, and who was found wandering in the woods. Through an organized, systematic schedule of lessons, Itard tried to educate the young boy, with a mixture of successes and failures.

One friend in a l'Arche community in Ireland said that her father was scared when he heard she was going to be an assistant in this religious community with people who are mentally retarded: The father was scared that she would possibly be raped and brutalized by "these people." Television shows like "Life Goes On" and movies like *Best Boy* both focus on a broader, and therefore complex, realistic portrayal of people with the disabling condition of mental retardation. Yet we still struggle with what and how to talk about the condition that, for the lack of a better name, we say is "mental retardation."

This definition is truly representative of the fluctuating history of labels and categories. Since 1921 there have been nine revisions of the definition of "mental retardation." The most common definition for mental retardation was written by the American Association on Mental Retardation (AAMR) in 1992:

> Mental Retardation refers to substantial limitations in present functioning. It is characterized by significantly subaverage intellectual functioning, existing concurrently with related limitations in two or more of the following applicable adaptive skill areas: communication, self-care, home living, social skills, community use, self-direction, health and safety, functional academics, leisure, and work. Mental retardation manifests before age 18.[39]

When referring to "subaverage intellectual functioning," what health care professionals are looking at is the ability people with mental retardation have in tasks such as writing, reading, math, communicating, and even computer skills. To find out how well a child or an adult is able to function, the special educator is looking at the ability to perhaps read and comprehend a story in a book, or to write a letter to a friend. If the child is not able to read and write on the same level as most other children of the same age and educational background, and the child is having a very hard time even keeping up with these activities, then there may be reason to be concerned about how well the child is functioning intellectually.

When talking about a person's "adaptive skills," health care professionals are referring to is the ability to respond and act in a socially normal or appropriate manner, given the context of the social situation. For example, when walking into a fellowship or coffee time after worship, a person who is mentally retarded may not talk to anyone but just sit and drink juice and eat doughnuts on the floor. Or the adult who is mentally retarded may voluntarily go to the front of a church when the children are invited to come for a children's sermon. Overall, the adult or child who is mentally retarded is unable to conform or change and respond appropriately in various social settings; they appear incapable of negotiating the different social settings they experience in life, being verbally loud in quiet places and whispering and acting shy when shouting is fine.

When writing that mental retardation "manifests before age 18," professionals believe that those with the condition are developmentally behind others of the same age in completing certain activities before 18 years old. For example, the child who may be mentally retarded is unable to walk a balance beam or turn a somersault by a certain age. Another example is that adolescents with mental retardation may not be able to comprehend certain abstract concepts, like "grace," or do certain mathematical functions in their head, choosing to work them out in a more concrete fashion by counting on their fingers.

It is important to remember that before anyone is diagnosed as being "mentally retarded" he or she must show an intellectual impairment, socially maladaptive behavior, and developmental problems all at the same time. Each one of the above three descriptions, if considered alone, could also be a result of other problems that are not connected to mental retardation but are due to some other disabling condition. An intellectual impairment like an inability for someone to read may also be a learning disability or a visual impairment; socially maladaptive behavior may be due to emotional disabilities; and developmental problems may be due to physical impairments.

Another important distinction is that while some children and adults may look like they are mentally retarded, many others do not look mentally retarded. As an example, children and adults with Down's syndrome *look* like they are mentally retarded as well as act it according to professional consideration. Others *look* "normal" but, due to a toxic agent like alcohol, which may lead to fetal alcohol syndrome, or to a virus like rubella (German measles), may have all of the characteristics of someone who is mentally retarded.

Because a child or an adult has mental retardation, this does not mean that they cannot learn many things in life. The true limitation appears to be dependent on the culture or the community in which the person who is mentally retarded lives, not necessarily on his or her disability.

Learning Disabilities

There are some children in Christian religious education programs and in worship services that may seem especially slow and ill at ease in reading Scripture aloud because they fear they will mix words and letters around, or who get restless when asked to memorize a prayer, or who have very short attention spans when asked to write their ideas about a theological term. Because of their inability to read aloud, write, think, or memorize like others, the people with these problems may also think poorly of themselves, isolating themselves from peer groups in a religious gathering. Though these people are not mentally retarded, tasks that seem easy for others in the congregation seem impossible for them. The disabling condition that these people may have falls under the larger umbrella of "learning disabilities."

As accepted in the Public Law 94-142, the Education for All Handicapped Children Act, the definition is as follows:

> The term "children with specific learning disabilities" means those children who have disorders that are intrinsic to the individual and presumed to be due to central nervous system dysfunction, involved in understanding or in using language, spoken or written, which disorder may manifest itself in imperfect ability to listen, think, speak, read, write, spell, or to do mathematical calculations. Such disorders include such conditions as perceptual handicaps, brain injury, minimal brain dysfunction, dyslexia, and developmental aphasia. Such term does not include children who have learning problems which are primarily the result of visual, hearing, or motor handicaps, of mental retardation, of emotional disturbance, or of environmental, cultural or economic disadvantage.[40]

According to some special educators, this label is often changing and hard to tack down because one of the primary issues is knowing if a person has a learning disability due to mental retardation, emotional problems, or cultural problems, or if the learning disability is truly tied back to a problem in the central nervous system. Some research studies show that it is more prevalent among boys than girls, and that most learning-disabled children are of elementary school age, probably due to the way children with learning disabilities are assessed. For a while, it appeared that learning-disabled children came primarily from white, middle-class families, but this has changed in recent years as more children with learning disabilities come from minority groups and a lower socioeconomic background.[41]

There is a good chance that some children and adults in every congregation or parish may have a learning disability. You may suspect a learning disability if you notice the following characteristics: First, the person with a learning disability has a hard time reading and writing. Some children have a decoding or reading recognition problem, making sense of what is written and how it sounds; others have a hard time comprehending or understanding what a teacher is reading.

Second, because of their difficulty reading, comprehending, and writing in a Christian religious education activity, a teacher may also notice that they have an attention problem, probably due to boredom. Some children with learning disabilities also show a problem in just relating to other children, revealing some insecurity in social situations. Many children with learning disabilities have a poorer self-image than their peers. The child with a learning disability may also have problems in terms of short- and long-term memories.

Third, some children with a learning disability reveal that they have what is called a language deficit: They are not able to comprehend and use abstract rules for word combinations and basic grammar. They do not seem to have an innate knowledge of how to make words and ideas flow together. Thus, in telling stories and narratives, an important aspect of being a part of a church, people with learning disabilities may often be lost.

Communication and Language Disorders

The American Speech-Language-Hearing Association (ASHA) defined communication disorders as "impairments in articulation, language, voice or fluency." This includes hearing impairments in the definition when they impeded "the development, performance, or maintenance of articulation, language, voice, or fluency.[42]

Speech disorders involve both the perception of the listener as well as the characteristic of the disordered behavior itself. "Speech is abnormal when it deviates so far from the speech of other people that it calls attention to itself, interferes with communication, or causes the speaker or his listener to be distressed."[43]

A language disorder is as follows:

> A language disorder is the abnormal acquisition, comprehension or expression of spoken or written language. Individuals with language disorders frequently have problems in sentence processing or in abstracting information meaningfully for storage and retrieval from short and long term memory (ASHA).

Some people with communication disorders struggle with specific words and word orders, along with articulation of specific sounds to relay their thoughts and feelings. For example, some people stutter over certain words. One of the biblical characters from the Old Testament, Moses, was considered to have a language disorder (Exodus 4:10):

> But Moses said to the Lord, "O my Lord, I have never been eloquent, neither in the past nor even now that you have spoken to your servant; but I am slow of speech and slow of tongue."

Others with disordered speech may have good language but are unable to produce certain letters, so that a "t" sounds like a "d," or an "s" sounds like a "z." Others will substitute letters like "w" for "r," so that "really" is pronounced "weally."

In some other cases, people with communication disorders may have a problem with the quality of their voice, sounding very nasal or very hoarse, while others have problems with the pitch of their voice, being either too high, too low, or too monotonous.

Many communication disorders may be a result of other disabling conditions. For example, some children or adults with cerebral palsy, a physical disability, may have some speech and language problems due to problems with the central nervous system and an inability to control posture and breathing. For others, communication disorders may be a result of mental retardation or a learning disability. And in some cases, the communication disorder is due to the family environment, where, for example, a child constantly hears a certain word mispronounced.

Again, there is a good chance that children and adults with communication disorders will be part of a church's life. And language plays an important part in the life of these communities; the language of a child is one of the ways to determine if he or she has a disabling condition.

Hearing Impairment

Many times, a person with a hearing impairment baffles a hearing person. I have seen and heard many hearing people talking loudly or shouting to a person with a hearing impairment, or turning away their face, or speaking so slowly that their meaning is lost. Many people with hearing impairments are also baffled by these efforts at communication.

What is a hearing impairment? A definition used among healthcare professionals is as follows:

A deaf person is one whose hearing is disabled to an extent . . . that precludes the understanding of speech through the ear alone, with or without the use of a hearing aid.

A hard-of-hearing person is one whose hearing is disabled to an extent . . . that makes difficult, but does not preclude, the understanding of speech through the ear alone, with or without a hearing aid.[44]

A person with a hearing impairment is hard to visually spot in a community unless there are overt signs like a hearing aid. Some people who are deaf rely on sign language, a manual method using one's hands and fingers. American Sign Language is such a manual or physical method of communicating, with its own grammar and syntax, which is different from English grammar.

Some people with hearing impairments use what is known as an oralist or auralist path, depending totally on spoken language and lip-reading. For those with residual hearing, there is a combination of amplified sound with the use of a hearing aid fitted into the ear, lipreading, and speech itself to obtain communication skills. In this method, lipreading, the visual interpretation of spoken communication by reading the speaker's lips, encourages the deaf person who wants to keep in meaningful contact with the hearing world. Thus, a person who lipreads will need to see the face, especially the mouth, of the speaker.

One other pattern of communication has been cued speech. With this method the hearing speaker's hand is held up near the mouth so that the fingers can perform special signs, or cues, that, in turn, substitute for sounds that are not easily lipread.[45] This is a new way of communicating in many American public school systems.

Some people with hearing impairments use what is known as total communication, the act of speaking and signing English at the same time, often with the use of residual hearing. This is a combination of finger spelling, sign language like ASL, speech or lipreading, speech, and auditory amplification. The idea behind total communication is that a person who has a hearing impairment will be able to use one of the above methods of communication to express their ideas and communicate with another person.[46]

There are some political issues that need to be recognized. In some mainline church denominations, such as the Evangelical Lutheran Church in America and the Episcopal Church in America, congregations are attended by and open to those who primarily use manual language like sign language. There are many people with hearing impairments in other religious gatherings, especially those with members who are chronologically older than "average." As with the other disabling conditions, what the community—both those who are the hearing members and those with hearing impairments—will need to work on is exploring the various approaches for communicating. While some parishes adopt the manual method of communicating, hiring someone to use sign language in worship services, congregations need to remember that this is only one among many approaches and methods in communicating with those who have a hearing impairment.

Both the journalist Henry Kisor and the neuropsychologist Oliver Sacks identified the cultural and political issues that need to be considered in working with people who are hearing impaired, as there may be one community of people with hearing impairments that use sign language while another uses oral communication.[47] In the middle of all this comes the parishioners who just want to live with those who may have a hearing impairment. To know which method of communication the person with a hearing impairment uses and adapt to it may be the most prudent path toward welcoming those with hearing impairments.

Visual Impairment

A visual impairment is a "handicap of mobility" as much as it is a disabling condition that affects an individual's ability to physically and sensorily negotiate a changing world.[48] While it is a handicap of mobility, it may also be an unobtrusive and nonthreatening disabling condition as it is so widespread in America, yet no one seems to realize that they have it.

For example, when addressing a group about the presence of people with disabilities, I will sometimes begin the lecture with the question, "Who here has a disabling condition of any sort?" Even when I am addressing people who are wearing eyeglasses or contact lenses, these people will not raise their hands, until I point out that they are wearing an adaptive device to help them see more clearly. Glasses are not only a stylistic addition to one's fashion ensemble: More importantly, they point to a need that some people have in order to see more clearly.

People with visual problems can also be very easy to spot in a crowd as they may be using a white cane to guide them, they may be using a guide dog, or they may be holding onto someone's arm as a guide through a crowded room. Like people with a hearing impairment, people with visual impairments, like blindness, even have their own language. The use of braille, a special coded language, makes it possible for people who are blind to read and write.

A visual impairment is defined as follows:

> (Someone) whose visual impairment interferes with his optimal learning and achievement, unless adaptations are made in the methods of presenting learning experiences, the nature of the materials used, and/or in the learning environment.[49]

A person who is blind is one whose vision is 20/200 or less, even with correction. Roughly, this means that a person can only see at 20 feet what someone else with average sight can see at 200 feet.[50] This doesn't mean that the person can't see at all. They can still sense brightness and darkness of light with some residue of visual sight.

There is little that a person with a visual impairment cannot do that a sighted person can do; the only difference is usually the adaptive devices or equipment that may be needed in order to take in and express thoughts and feelings. The person with a visual impairment may need to use braille, a system of touch reading developed in 1829 by a blind Frenchman, Louis Braille. It is a series of different combinations of dots on a piece of heavy manila paper, ready from left to right, with both hands, one leading while the other follows. A person can read from a braille text, as well as write in braille using a braille typewriter or braille-writer.[51]

In walking around and negotiating the physical space of their environment, people with a visual impairment are dependent on their other bodily senses. One popular thought has been that a person with a visual impairment has better use of the other senses, such as touch or kinesthetic movement, smell, and hearing. Many people with visual impairments have learned to use and rely on these other senses to negotiate their environments.

To help people with visual impairments move around more easily, some parishes have made public telephones accessible, placed certain wall fixtures that can be detected with a cane, placed handrails throughout a building, and placed larger signs, sometimes in braille, throughout sanctuaries. Much of the reading information distributed congregation has been an attempt to also communicate with people who are visually impaired by using braille and large-print hymn books, Bibles, and bulletins. Some institutions, such as public schools, are also using models or tactile maps that represent the spatial relationships that people can master through touch. Keeping a room's furniture in the same place does help the person who is visually impaired who has already mapped out a room in his or her own mind.

One last thing that I have noticed among the seeing population: There is the hidden assumption that a person who cannot see cannot hear. A key concept for a person who is non-disabled is learning to assist a person with a disabling condition such as a hearing impairment: Let the person who is disabled tell you what he or she needs; don't assume that you, the non-disabled person, automatically know.

Behavior Problems

One of the first times that I worked with children with behavioral problems was as a music therapy student. I was asked to work in a school with two young boys, Brian and his friend Sean, both eight years old. I was told that they were having a hard time concentrating on their schoolwork, but no one told me in what fashion this "concentration" problem would manifest itself. The first day I worked with these boys, they could not sit down. It was physically impossible for them to sit, as they had such short attention spans. Instead, for the 30 minutes I was with them, they ran around an otherwise empty classroom, ripping paper off of the bulletin board. A simple "Please sit down!" got no response whatsoever from either boy. Later, I was told by the teacher that these boys were "hyperactive," a condition that falls under the area of behavioral problems.

According to the Education For All Handicapped Children Act, Public Law 94-142, serious emotional disturbance or behavioral disorders, terms that are interchanged, are defined as follows:

> The term means a condition exhibiting one or more of the following characteristics over a long period of time to a marked degree, which adversely affects educational performance:
> 1. an inability to learn which cannot be explained by intellectual, sensory, or health factors;
> 2. an inability to build or maintain satisfactory interpersonal relationships with peers and teachers;

3. inappropriate behavior or feelings under normal circumstances;
4. a general pervasive mood of unhappiness or depression;
5. a tendency to develop physical symptoms or fears associated with personal or school problems.

This term may include children who are schizophrenic or autistic. The term does not include children who are socially maladjusted unless it is determined that they are seriously emotionally disturbed. [52]

In this case, the definition of a behavior problem or emotional disturbance depends on the action of the person, who the person is, and the setting where the behavior occurs. In other words, what a behavioral problem is depends upon the perception of the educator or parent and the person who is having the problem.

In the above list, the first description focuses on the problem the child has in learning. This would be a child who is often unable to sit in one place and work on her math problem and is roaming around the room whenever possible. Or it could be the child who sits in a chair not willing to lift his head off the desk to answer a question from a Sunday School workbook.

The second description focuses on the child who is unable to maintain a personal relationship with any of the other children or a Christian religious educator. For example, a child may continually lie or undermine relationships among other children, failing to follow through on commitments and responsibilities in a youth group. A child who is hostile, malicious, or cruel with few guilty feelings may have an emotional problem.

In describing the adolescent who displays "inappropriate behavior or feelings," the third description, perhaps an adolescent is too ready to throw a punch at another child for an inoffensive, silly remark; or an angry child settles differences with others by throwing an object, such as a chair, at a youth leader.

The fourth characteristic focuses on one who is in a continual state of unhappiness or depression, such as an adult who is nearly always depressed to the point of threatening suicide or displaying self-abusive behavior such as hitting one's head against a wall. Some children, adolescents, and adults may experience anxiety that leads to their depression because they feel isolated and helpless, unwanted by others in their world.

The last description centers on children with hypochondriac-like tendency, based on certain fears. Some children with emotional problems may display fears of personal or school problems by not being able to talk at all in certain circumstances around certain people in school, or they may weep uncontrollably before going to a certain activity or even when thinking of a certain person. Others may be overdependent and easily depressed, acting shy and submissive, never questioning but accepting what anyone tells him or her to do in a group of children, no matter how injurious the child's actions are.

Chances are, each one of us has felt some of these feelings at one time or another in our lives. The real problem arises when these reactions are more than just a mind game, part of our imagination, and, instead, become part of our lifestyle—a regular pattern for how we resolve conflicts and problems in our lives. In this case, simply put, we do not merely have emotional or behavioral problems that we can control; the emotional or behavioral problems control us.

Many people with these problems—children, adolescents, and adults alike—may enter into the life of our Christian religious education program and come to our youth groups, while many sit with us when churches gather for worship. Some people with emotional and behavioral problems have them under control enough that they are able to be a part of the activities but for others, just sitting in worship or joining in a youth group while controlling behavior may be quite a task.

Many ask why people have behavioral and emotional problems. Some theories suggest that the problem is biological and physical, and that the afflicted person has little control. Other theorists suggest that it is due to environmental factors or causes, such as family problems between parents and children.[53]

In many congregations and parishes, the one thing that has been learned in special education programs that may be easily transferred is working on finding out who these people are. There are times that a person with a behavioral problem will be able to function in a large group. But a Christian religious educator, a youth leader, or a pastor may want to be sure that, between the person with a behavioral problem and the religious community, there is someone who can help out in times of emergency.

Multiple and Severe Disabilities

Some people have more than one disabling condition. In fact, in looking at the conditions we've discussed so far, one disabling condition may be the cause of another disabling condition. For example, people born with Down's Syndrome may also have some physical and physiological problems, such as cardiac problems. Or those with cerebral palsy, a neuromuscular condition, may have a language or communication disorder due to their physical problems. If a person is mentally retarded and categorized as also having an emotional problem, this question may follow: Did the mental retardation cause the emotional problem, or did the emotional problem bring on the mental retardation? Sometimes a disabling condition is not easy to isolate under just one label and category; many times, people have multiple disabling conditions.

This is why there is the following categorization for people who have multiple disabling conditions. The following term was adopted in 1974 by the U.S. Office of Education, now the U.S. Department of Education:

> Severely handicapped children are those who because of the intensity of their physical, mental, or emotional problems need educational, social, psychological, and medical services beyond those which are traditionally offered by regular and special education programs, in order to maximize participation in society and self-fulfillment. Such severely handicapped children may possess severe language or perceptual-cognitive deprivation and evidence a number of abnormal behaviors including failure to attend to even the most pronounced stimuli, self-mutilation, manifestations of durable and intense temper tantrums, and the absence of even the most rudimentary forms of verbal control. They may also have extremely fragile physiological conditions.[54]

In other words, these are children who, often due to problems associated with their birth, have more than one disabling condition. Sometimes a mother will use a drug such as alcohol, and the child may be born with fetal alcohol syndrome, resulting in physical deformities as well as mental retardation.[55] Or a lack of oxygen during the birth process itself may cause irreversible destruction of brain cells, resulting in mental retardation and, maybe, cerebral palsy.

A child with multiple and severe disabling conditions will need a great deal of physical and sensory stimulation, which the family can provide. But the family will also need some intervention involving the support of their community network, including their church to meet the demanding needs of their child.[56]

A disabling condition that will be stressful on the life of the family is autism, which falls under the large umbrella of multiple and severe disabling conditions. In 1979, the National Society for Autistic Children affirmed this description of autism:

> Autism is a severely incapacitating life-long developmental disability which usually appears during the first three years of life. It occurs in approximately five out of 10,000 births and is four times more common in boys than in girls. It has been found throughout the world in families of all racial, ethnic, and social backgrounds.[57]

Children with autism are known for having a hard time relating to other people, fixating on certain objects in a room and showing flat emotional responses in some situations. They are in strong need of a highly structured, overly repetitive mannerism.

For example, take Joey, a five-year-old boy who is autistic. Joey rocks to and fro in place, smiling and rocking for a good hour. Suddenly, while he rocks, he shouts, "Joey wants to hit, Joey wants to hit!" and then goes and repeatedly hits his head on a wall or on a desk until he is stopped by one of the adults in the room. Then he walks around the room, crying, until someone holds and rocks him.

One story that I heard from a mother with an autistic son demonstrates what can happen sometimes in congregational life. The mother, one Sunday, brought her child to worship as she couldn't find anyone to sit with the child in the nursery. The son, who was four, had never responded to much of any stimulus in the world, always rocking or twirling when he would sit down. But in the beginning of the worship service, when the organ played its first chord for the prelude, the child stopped rocking, looked up, smiled, and was still for a few minutes: It was one of the first moments when the child seemed to show awareness of the surrounding environment.

Physical Disabilities and Health Impairments

My friend Lucy has cerebral palsy, a physical disability that is caused by damage to the motor control center of her brain. As she explains it, her mind sends mixed messages to different body parts: She will tell herself to reach out for the salt on the table while her brain is also receiving a garbled message telling it *not* to pick up the salt, thus producing the shaking effect of her arm while reaching to pass the salt. The condition influences her muscular well-being, getting in the way of such simple, voluntary motion, as taking the paper wrapping off a straw, or more complex motions, such as typing.

I have a friend whose name is Tom. He's in a wheelchair due to cerebral palsy. He needs some assistance in doing things like taking a bath or shower; he depends on a hotel to have rails in the bathroom so that he can independently maneuver himself at the end of a long day of speaking engagements.

Physical disabilities are, according to some statistics, the smallest group of disabling conditions. According to the special educators Samuel Kirk and James Gallagher, a physical disability is "a condition that interferes with the child's ability to use his or her body . . . like an orthopedic impairment. . . . A condition that requires ongoing medical attention is a health impairment."[58] Physical disabilities include artificial limbs that leave a person unable to write with a pen, walk, or use conventional bathrooms. Other physical impairments include amputations, the removal of a limb, and arthritis, an inflammation of the body's joints.

Like a person with a visual impairment, a person with a physical disability may have a condition that is visible to other people, by the use of a wheelchair, a cane, or some other adaptive equipment that helps the person to maneuver. Some people with physical disabilities depend on the help of others, while others believe there is a time to help and a time to wait to be asked to help.

Health impairments include such conditions as asthma, cystic fibrosis, heart defects, cancer, diabetes, leukemia, muscular dystrophy, and hemophilia, to name but a few. These conditions impair a person's participation in a parish, a Christian religious education activity, or in any other group in the church.

Under this umbrella of disabling conditions, I have worked with many children with epilepsy, a neurological disorder where the brain sends out a spontaneous burst of neural transmissions, thus causing a seizure, resulting in some loss of consciousness.

The other disabling condition I have seen more often among children is leukemia. A child with leukemia is not getting enough white cells in the blood system to fight infections.

Other adolescents and adults in the parish may be coping with health impairments from cancer to heart defects, diabetes to asthma. All of these conditions cannot help but interfere with how people feel about and look at themselves. They may also interfere with participation in Christian religious education programs and worship, as a person with a health impairment will struggle with pain and fatigue during long-term medical treatment.

Talking to and Being with "Them" At God's Banquet

This chapter's focus has been on the cautious use of labels and categories. But the question for congregations and parishes, asked of minister or priest, Christian religious educator or lay leader, is: "Are labels and categories really necessary within the context of the Christian community?" While the surrounding culture, living perhaps by the hidden, normative standard so well described by Nicholas Hobbs, has marked certain people as being disabled, does the Church live and organize life by a different standard? Is the Church called to be a different community of "resident aliens"?[59] How much does our belief in being created in the image of God influence how we perceive and interact with others in our respective Christian communities?

In this focus on labeling and categorizing people's limitations, it is important to remember that not one of these labels tells or reveals much about the *person* with the disabling condition. A label hides the truth that not all people with mental retardation can do the same thing; not all people with visual impairments think the same way; and not all people with autism experience the world in the same way. As Henry Kisor suggests, "homogenizing the deaf in one way is like assuming all African-Americans vote Democratic in American politics."[60] Each person who happens to have a disabling condition has his or her own way of living, perceiving, and relating to and with others and God.

How then shall we look at, listen to, work, live, and worship with those whom society has labeled as disabled? On a television talk show a few years ago, the newspaper columnist George Will, whose son is mentally retarded due to Down's Syndrome, spoke about the very human nature of his child. As was stated in the previous chapter, many people try to make those with disabling conditions, like mental retardation, either Holy Innocents of God and blameless before the Creator,

or evil incarnate as a child of the devil. Will said that his son is h.
full of the same complex emotions, drives, and stressors as any ᴜᴛner
child. There are times that his son is joyful and spiteful, happy and
sad, sharing and greedy, loving and hating . . . all in all, the child is
human, nothing more and nothing less. Maybe the greatest way to
approach his son and others who also have some serious limitations
and wonderful gifts is as a human being.

In perceiving that other person as human, with a unique configuration of gifts and talents, abilities, and limitations, another important
theme is that congregations and parishes should not assume that they
will need to care for those with disabilities as objects of charity. Instead,
many people with disabling conditions are asking the Church to become physically, psychologically, intellectually, emotionally, and spiritually more flexible, with a spirit of adventure that welcomes each
person just as they are to their respective places of worship.

Another way to look at this issue of labeling is that the "they" in
the above description of labels and categories are "us." How should
Christian gatherings perceive those whom society has labeled and sub-
sequently categorized as being disabled or having a disabling condition?
People with disabling conditions are, first and foremost, people—human beings like all of us, with thoughts and feelings, opinions and
commentaries, needs and wants like others. As human beings, mere
mortals, we are all part of God's creative order, dependent on God for
our very lives and source of identity; knowledge of whose we are. As
human beings created in God's image, we all have the potential to
reflect the goodness of God. We also all have the capacity to sin and
turn away from God. In this sense, we are all broken, limited in our
ability to relate to one another and to God. Second, we are *all* born
with many things we can and cannot do, and all of us are dependent
on a particular community that needs and wants our abilities and sup-
ports and cares for our limitations. For example, the longer we live,
the more natural, physiological limits we will find. All people have
unrealized potential for new ways of living, relating, and being with
others. Placed in the right context, with the right people at the right
time, one may find one's potential gifts from just being part of the
Church realized. I have witnessed too many people who could not read
or write and were labeled "mentally retarded" or "autistic." But they
were amazingly gifted at painting a picture or playing the piano. And

some people with severe disabilities, by their mere presence, remind a congregation of the simple gifts of life.

For example, consider the story of Innocente, who was severely mentally retarded, in the l'Arche community in the Ivory Coast. She was never able to speak, walk, or grow much. She remained like a young child only a few months old. But, as Jean Vanier noticed:

> her eyes and whole body quiver with love whenever she is held in love; a beautiful smile unfolds in her face and her whole being radiates peace and joy. Innocente is not helped by ideas, no matter how deep or beautiful they may be; she does not need money or power of a job; she does not want to prove herself; all she wants is love, touch and communion. When she receives the gift of love, she quivers in ecstasy; if she feels abandoned, she closes herself up in inner pain—the poorer a person is . . . the more the cry is solely for communion and for friendship. The more then the heart of the person who hears the cry, and responds to it, is awoken.[61]

By no means am I arguing that Christians should ignore the serious limitations or special conditions that some people have due to some physical, mental, or emotional condition. What I am arguing for is that these disabling conditions be put in a perspective that will differ greatly from the norms used by other helping professions. The perspective that I am choosing to look at is based on the story of God's amazing love for all of creation.

The theologian Stanley Hauerwas rightly understands that people with disabilities such as mental retardation remind us that *their* condition is *our* condition insofar as we are all faithful followers of Christ.[62] For example, including people with disabilities at the Eucharistic meal, one of the central communal sacraments of the Church, reminds us all that we are present at this table not because our good works got us a place there, but because God has called all of us there. God calls us just as we are, in our vulnerable, broken, and wounded condition, to come and receive God's love, sharing and being nourished by the body and blood of the risen Lord (see Chapter 8).

Bringing together both people with disabilities and those who are non-disabled around the Lord's table is a powerful symbol of reconciliation. It becomes the place where people may drop their fears and hostilities, overcoming the "we–they" barrier. The scholar Margaret Visser understands that the very act of eating together helps people get over fights and differences. The action of eating together can ritu-ally express what is shared, held, and enjoyed in common, which, in the case of the Church, is the gift of love given by God in Christ.[63]

In the following chapter I will describe in further detail what has been the method of caring for people with disabling conditions from both a biblical and historical reference. It is helpful, in finally coming to a new way of perceiving and speaking with people with disabling conditions in various religious communities, to look at the past and the present stories of how Jews and Christians alike have related to them.

3

• • •

A Brief History
and Theological Reflection
on the Place and Presence
of People with Disabilities

People with "disabling conditions" have been present in our world
for more than just this century. Issues surrounding how best to
care for, work with, cure, and live with others who are disabled has
challenged all human communities throughout the ages. In darker
times of human civilization, such as the city–states of ancient Greece
or Hitler's Nazi Germany, thousands and millions of people with some
kind of disabling condition were killed in the belief that wiping out
everyone with a specific disabled "gene," (the eugenic movement)
would prevent future malformations in the human race.

There are those today who believe that many disabling conditions
can be prevented if we discover the mysterious "magic bullet" to eradi-
cate endogenous or innate causes for certain disabling conditions.
These endogenous causes can be a single gene, such as the one causing
Down's syndrome or Fragile X Syndrome. There are also those who
look at the exogenous or outside causes of many of our disabling conditions, believing if we could only tinker with social and environmental
conditions, many disabling conditions would vanish.[64]

This book is not about either curing or eradicating disabling conditions, nor is it about relabeling and recategorizing people. Instead, the

book's focus is on discovering ways of reenvisioning people with disabling conditions with the hope of incorporating those who may have been denied a place within the active lives of our parishes and congregations, God's Banquet Feast on earth. For it is in the midst of Christ's community that all people find the loving support and liberty to be the people God created them to be.

In order to get a sense of what churches should and could do in inviting, welcoming, and accepting people with disabling conditions into our Christian gatherings, it is helpful to have some understanding and learn from our ancestors what has already been tried in the past. We will briefly look at historical and theological explanations of disabling conditions in hopes that we will gain some understanding of what has already been tried, so that we will not repeat the same mistake twice. And from the past, we may even find some clues as how best to welcome people with disabling conditions into our religious communities.

This chapter will briefly cover how the Jewish and Christian communities have reacted to and perceived those with disabling conditions, given their respective understanding of God's providence and relationship with humankind. In looking at the unfolding story of the children of Israel and the Christian Church in the context of God's story, we may gain some insight as to how and why these respective communities of faith responded the way that they have to those with disabling conditions.

This historical and theological summary is by no means exhaustive; it is meant to provide some basic understanding of the struggle religious communities have had in searching for a reason as to why certain people are born with, or later are struck by, a disabling condition. This broad historical and theological perspective will also help make a case for why the presence and participation of people who happen to have a disabling condition are essential for the life of our religious communities.

The Human Condition and the Disabling Conditions

Disabling conditions are nothing new to the human race. In anthropological and archeological studies of the human race, there is physical evidence that men and women have walked and grazed on this earth for over four million years. The historian Richard Scheerenberger writes that there were probably over one million people during prehistoric times who roamed throughout Africa and parts of the Western world as we know it.[65] During this time, it is probably safe to assume that they suffered many illnesses and diseases that we still experience today, due to everything from changes in weather to rough living conditions.

Scheerenberger describes that it was around 7000 B.C.E. that human beings pursued new ways of caring for those who were ill with the help of a medicine man or shaman. The shaman was called upon to exorcise any evil spirits that were afflicting a person. To cure people, the shaman used a variety of methods: magical powers, amulets, and good-luck objects. Some also used trephining, the removal of a small circular section of the skull bone from the top of the head, allowing the evil spirits causing a disability, such as epilepsy or a mental illness, to be freed.[66]

Later in the Near East, in the Babylonian empire during 1700 to 560 B.C.E., having a disability was perceived as a punishment by the gods or a sign of being possessed by evil spirits. All illnesses were a result of sin; and sin could be defined broadly, from such behavior as "spitting into a canal, the dipping of feet into unclean water, and the unnecessary handling of the sick."[67]

Babylonians also used fetuses for predicting the future, a practice called "fetomancy." For example, the birth of a child with an excess size or number of certain body parts—like a baby with six toes on each foot—would be a sign that the world would be injured.[68]

In Egypt, starting at or around 2850 B.C.E., the first dynasty was founded. This was a society that was largely controlled by priests on religious issues of life and death, as can be seen in many of the religious artifacts found within the great pyramids of ancient Egypt. Again, they believed that any disabling condition or illness was due to evil spirits, and sold amulets and charms to assure spiritual and physical healing.

Before Jesus' birth, persons who were mentally retarded were killed by the Spartan Greek society. Greek philosophers stated that the laws of nature dictated that only the fittest survive, so the society may have been applying natural law to prevent racial degeneration through the cessation of those considered defective. In Roman society, people who were mentally retarded were used by the wealthy to perform as fools or jesters. While those who were mentally retarded were tolerated by the Romans as diversions or amusements, there is no documentation of any effort to assist them.[69]

In the Beginning, When God Created . . . People with Disabilities in the Jewish Community

In the Priestly account, or first story of creation, in Genesis 1:1–2:4a, it is written that "God created humankind in his image, in the image of God he created them; male and female he created them" (Genesis 1:27, NRSV). Many have read this passage literally, not metaphorically: they believe that since we have arms, legs, noses, mouths, and ears, so must our image of God. This is reinforced in passages in the Bible where God is moving, walking, singing, and listening to Adam and Eve (Gen. 3:8). The theologian Burton Cooper states that we come to think of God as having a human face, sometimes adopting Michelangelo's famous painting of God creating Adam.[70]

The problem in understanding this language literally and not metaphorically is that it reinforces an understanding of God as literally having eyes, ears, mouth, and tongue. But God does not necessarily have eyes nor ears nor legs. These are all metaphors used to help us understand God's capacity to know us.[71]

Instead, to be created in the image of God means that humankind was created with the potential creative use of power, and with freedom within limits, which are both necessary for the human creatures to do all that God wants them to do.[72] The Creator God truly delighted in the creation-creature, wanting to live in a relationship that was based on a free, gracious commitment and invitation.[73]

The issue of being able bodied or having a disabling condition is not a significant part of the creation stories. Instead, what is significant is what happens in Genesis 3. When Adam and Eve are thrown out of the Garden of Eden, their collective punishment for turning away from God and eating the fruit from the tree of knowledge, is banishment to a world of mortality, not immortality; a world of pain, not of continual bliss; a world of weaknesses and severe limitations, not of abilities and seemingly limitless boundaries.

What is interesting in this story is that even though Eve and Adam break God's command not to eat of the tree of knowledge (Gen. 2:17), God still lets them live. The biblical scholar Walter Brueggemann understands that God, seeing the tension and anxiety of the human creatures who are unable to come to God themselves to confess what they did, does not kill them, even though physical limitations and death are now part of living on earth.[74]

In the early history of the people of Israel, there appears to be at least two different perspectives on care for and treatment of people with disabilities. On the one hand, we have the scriptural heritage that lacks the benefit of our present knowledge of the abilities of persons with disabilities. For example, the Judaic Deuteronomic law was strict about what would be offered on the sacrificial altar in worship of God. An animal with a blemish of any kind might not be offered to God (Lev. 22:22). A person with a blemish of any kind would also be unable to present an offering to God:

> The Lord spoke to Moses, saying: Speak to Aaron and say: No one of your offspring throughout their generations who has a blemish may approach to offer the food of his God. For no one who has a blemish shall draw near, one who is blind or lame, or one who has a mutilated face or a limb too long, or one who has a broken foot or a broken hand, or a hunch back, or a dwarf, or a man with a blemish in his eyes or an itching disease to scabs or crushed testicles. No descendant of Aaron the priest who has a blemish shall come near to offer the Lord's offerings by fire; since he has a blemish, he shall not come near to offer the food of his God. He may eat the food of his God, of the most holy as well as of the holy. But he shall not come near the curtain or approach the altar, because he has a blemish, that he may not profane my sanctuaries; for I am the Lord; I sanctify them. Thus Moses spoke to Aaron and to his sons and to all the people of Israel (Lev. 21:16–24, NRSV).

In this passage, we read of God the monarch, a king who will be served only by those who are considered clean, without blemish of any visible kind. It is apparent that one who is disabled is seen as being less than perfect, less than whole. The attitude toward those with disabilities among the children of Israel also reflects the predominant views of the Babylonians and the Egyptians of the time. What this passage from Leviticus and the cultic law reveals to the reader and hearer is a God who desires perfection in all ways by those who serve and worship Him in the holy places of Israel.

On the other hand, other passages also reveal that people with disabling conditions, with "blemishes," are not to be excluded from the ritualistic life of the children of Israel. "He [the one with a disability] may eat of the food of his God, of the most holy as well as of the holy" (Lev. 21:22, NRSV). People with disabling conditions are included as significant members of this group of pilgrims. Those who are able bodied are given special instructions to care for and treat everyone as equally important among the gathering of the children of Israel. This is because God told them so. The Deuteronomic writer, who probably recorded what we read in both the books of Leviticus and Deuteronomy, makes it clear that no one should make it harder for the children of Israel who are disabled, as we find in these passages: "'Cursed be anyone who misleads a blind person on the road. All the people shall say, 'Amen'" (Deut. 27:18, NRSV). And there is another passage like it:

> "You shall not revile the deaf or put a stumbling block before the blind; you shall fear your God: I am the Lord" (Lev. 19:14, NRSV).

In reading these passages, we come to understand another important characteristic about the relationship between God and the Israelites: Along with the other commandments of how to live in right relationship with God and neighbor, we read in both of these books, which reflect the moral code that the Israelites are to live by, that God cares so much for people with disabling conditions in the midst of and part of God's chosen people that the rest of the children of Israel are to make a place and allowances for those who are blind, deaf, or have diseases like leprosy (see also Leviticus 13 and 14).

This shows that God desires a relationship with all of the Israelites, making a place for the able and disabled within and among the chosen. Much of the Old Testament portrays a God who understands and desires justice and peace with this creation. As we find out in reading even the dramatic story of Job, God alone is Creator, mindful and considerate of the needs of all creation, even those whom society labels as being "disabled."

This theme of God caring for all those who are chosen, regardless of their abilities or limitations, is reflected in the writings of the Talmud as we read of God's relationship with humanity. Rabbi Abba bar Yudan said, "All that God has declared to be unclean in animals, God has pronounced desirable in men [sic]." Rabbi Alexandri is to have said: "If a private person uses broken vessels, it is a disgrace to him, but God uses broken vessels."[75]

These readings from Deuteronomy and Leviticus, along with the readings from the Talmud, suggest that people with disabling conditions are truly among the chosen of God. This is reaffirmed in Isaiah 43:8. In this passage the Lord, the "One who created you. . . . he who formed you," calls the people of Israel, saying not to fear God, who has called each person by name, "you are mine" (Isaiah 43:1). We read of God gathering the people back together from Babylonian captivity, promising to restore and protect the people. Among the people are those who are disabled:

> Bring forth the people who are blind, yet have eyes, who are deaf, yet have ears! Let all the nations gather together and let the peoples assemble . . . You are my witnesses, says the Lord, and my servant whom I have chosen, so that you may know and believe me and understand that I am he. Before me no god was formed, nor shall there be any after me. (Isaiah 43:9,10, NRSV).

God claims that those who are disabled, using the example of those with visual and hearing impairments, are brought together with all the children of Israel to be witnesses and servants of God. All are brought together in order to bring forth God's reign. The chosen people worship this God of justice, not as a condition to be sought, but as active participants in the unfolding story of God's creative acts on earth. In citing specifically those who are disabled in this passage from Isaiah, we read of a God who, throughout human history, is an advocate on behalf of people in need. God's sense of justice is biased and prejudiced, purely subjective; God has defended people with disabilities among the chosen.

People with Disabilities in the Christian Community Story

The image of God as the Creator, Redeemer, and Liberator who sides with those who are oppressed and barely living on the margins of society is given new expression in the life ministry of Jesus of Nazareth. According to all four gospel accounts, Jesus continually kept company and surrounded himself with the outcasts of Jewish society, including those with disabling conditions. The Gospel accounts of Matthew, Mark, Luke, and John are full of parables and situations where Jesus is living among those whom, even today, we would call disabled. For example, there is the parable of the great banquet table surrounded by people with disabilities (Luke 14:15–24), or the woman with the internal hemorrhaging who believes that Jesus can heal her wounds (Mark 5:34), or the man to whom Jesus gives sight, even though the Pharisees and disciples believe the blindness is just retribution for a sin in the man's family (John 9:1–34).

Three lessons that all may learn from Jesus' relationship with those with disabling conditions are as follows:

First, Jesus surrounds himself with those who are overtly or visibly disabled; Jesus knows how to *be with* those who are disabled. For example, there is the chaotic scene recorded in the Gospel of Luke, 7:18–23, where two messengers from John the Baptist go to ask Jesus, "Are you the one who is to come, or are we to wait for another?" They find Jesus *in the midst of people with disabilities,* healing them, talking with them, curing them of all kinds of diseases. Jesus is not afraid of those with disabilities, but chooses to *be with* those considered outcasts.

Second, in the midst of this scene of chaos, with people probably shoving one another to get closer to Jesus, the core of the gospel—the good news—is revealed. People with disabling conditions are primary in this revelatory scene:

> "Go and tell John what you have seen and heard: the blind receive their sight, the lame walk, the lepers are cleansed, the deaf hear, the dead are raised, the poor have good news brought to them. And blessed is anyone who takes no offense at me" (Luke 7:22, 23, NRSV).

Here, Jesus is telling what will be the signs of the good news. But Jesus is not only telling the disciples of John what to look for; He is also *doing* the good news! In other words, Jesus is teaching and doing what he is preaching. The good news is that people who, both figuratively and literally, are disabled, will to be healed and made whole by the One who alone can perform this miracle, the Creator of life itself,

God. Jesus doesn't only *tell* these disciples about the Good News; He *is* the Good News.

Third, because Jesus so closely identifies with people who are disabled, either sitting with them, eating meals with them, curing some, or hugging and caring for others, this empathetic response to all who come to him displays a spirit of acceptance that few others had shown. All the gospel accounts are full of stories of Jesus' close identification and solidarity with those whom others had seen as worthless and devalued members of the human family.

The theologian Dorothee Soelle writes about this extraordinary ability that Jesus models for us in being able to identify with those who were sick or disabled; in a sense, for the sufferer's sake, Jesus also suffered. God in Christ healed these people of their brokenness and disabilities by taking on the wounds, tears, and aches of humanity.[76] Jesus also cries at the pain, the wounds of others, offering to take upon himself the burdens of humanity saying, "Come unto me, all who labor and are heavy laden, and I will give you rest. Take my yoke upon you, and learn from me; for I am gentle and humble in heart, and you will find rest for your souls" (Matthew 11:28, 29, NRSV).

This ability to take the wounds of others, to know the true value and hurt of being disabled in an able-bodied society, of knowing that one's limitations and abilities are all accepted, is, itself, a healing, curing act of love. It is also reflected in the passage from Matthew 8:17, where we read that Jesus Christ "fulfilled what was spoken by the prophet Isaiah: He took our infirmities and bore our diseases" (NRSV). Jesus is able to administer and give freely this gracious act of love because it is God in Christ who is greater than any individual. God's healing presence, acceptance of what the person can and cannot do, acceptance of who "I am," because of whose we are, brings forth hope in the life of those who believe in God.[77]

The Early Christians' Response to People with Disabilities

After the death and the resurrection of Jesus Christ, early Christians envisioned the Church as, according to the Apostle Paul, the living "body of Christ" (Romans 12), called to be a community of people who share in the common confession that Jesus Christ is Lord. A common image of the early Christian Church is a tightly knit fellowship, the first attempt to live a communal life as Christians. They tried to maintain a community where mutual aid was basic in collective life, feeding the hungry, clothing the needy, and caring for the ill or disabled, with the apostles healing many who were sick (Acts 4:32–35, NRSV). As we read in the Acts of the Apostles, the early church was overwhelmed by the needs of the people living in Jerusalem. Few of them had private property, and there were far too many who were hungry and homeless for the Church to meet all their needs.[78]

From those early times of the Christian Church, people with disabilities have either been cared for or, sometimes, abused by, many within the church. For example, in the early medieval ages, to be disabled was seen as a sign of grace among some Christians. The thought was that as Christ himself healed many of their illnesses and disabling conditions, so sickness became a way that one could be purified of one's sins. Disease is suffering and it is through suffering that humanity is completed by God's saving grace.[79]

As the person with a disability is one who has become a participant in God's grace, so too, caring for the disabled person in one's home was seen as one's Christian obligation. The person with a disability became a symbol of the wounded Christ who called for the follower to visit and care for the afflicted, based on this passage from the Gospel of Matthew:

> I was naked and you gave me clothing, I was sick and you took care of me, I was in prison and you visited me . . . And the king will answer them, "Truly, I tell you, just as you did it to one of the least of these who are members of my family, you did it to me" (Matthew 25:36,40, NRSV).

To take care of the person with a disabling condition within one's family became an opportunity to meet the needs of Christ for the caregiver as well.[80]

With the spread of Christianity and its underlying doctrine of compassion for the unfortunate for a while at least the plight of persons who were disabled improved; they were provided with clothing, food, and shelter. Some believed that the utterances of the person who was mentally retarded reflected their unique ability to communicate with the supernatural or were the revelations of heavenly infants of the good God.

However, as mentioned earlier, the future of some with disabling conditions was not necessarily bright. Using people who were mentally retarded as fools or jesters for the amusement of the household and its guests did not occur only in the Roman era, but also in the early Middle Ages of Europe. People who were mentally retarded also became the playthings of princes and the courts. Jesters were recruited from persons with physical disabilities and mental illnesses.[81] Even Pope Leo X's dinners, noted for fine food, had entertainment:

> Buffoons and jesters [who] were nearly always to be found at his table where the guests were encouraged to laugh at their antics and at the cruel jokes which were played on them—as when, for instance, some half-witted, hungry dwarf was seen guzzling a plate of carrion covered in a strong sauce under the impression that he was being privileged to consume the finest fare.[82]

Another option for those people who were mentally retarded or ill was to be taken into Christian hospitals that were founded throughout the Eastern Orthodox realm of Christendom during the 4th century, and later in the 5th century in Europe.[83] It was in the earlier part of the Middle Ages when the hospitals or hospices were established in Europe, usually by monastic orders. Fabiola, a 4th-century Roman matron, started a hospice in her home, as did St. Elizabeth of Hungary, who turned her castle into a Christian hospice for the poor.[84] The patron saint of the "feebleminded" was also regarded as the patron saint of all children, of sailors, and of pawnbrokers: Saint Nicholas Thaumaturgos, the Wonder-Worker. He was the 4th century bishop of Myra; now he is affectionately known as Santa Claus.[85]

In the 5th century, orders of Christians organized monasteries that were developed as hospices to extend and formalize Christian service to those who were ill. The Council of Carthage in 436 C.E. urged the bishops to begin and maintain Christian hospices in close proximity to cathedrals. This was in service to and for Christ, with prayer and free services their main themes.[86]

Relics and Pilgrimages
In the Care of People with
Disabling Conditions in Europe

In the history of the Church, one of the ways these hospitals and hospices for people with disabling conditions provided care was by using works of religious art as a method of healing. Like primitive men and women who used inanimate objects to heal the ill, people in the Church used religious objects such as religious paintings as a tool or vehicle for healing. Concerning religious objects, one has only to tour the cathedrals of Britain, France, and Italy to remember the importance of the relics of the members of the Christian church for the possible healing of people with various disabling conditions. Relics are the material remnants of a saint after his or her death, or any other object that had been in contact with the body of a particular martyr of the Church. The reason these relics had special attraction to many pilgrims throughout the ages is that the saints were thought to have been temples of the Holy Spirit of God. Pilgrims would walk for hundreds of miles to Canterbury, St. Albans, Chartres, and St. Peter's in hopes of being healed. Praying before a handkerchief that had been in touch with the Apostle Paul's body, perhaps celebrating the Eucharist over the bones of St. Peter, or praying at a church with a piece of cloth that maybe Mary, the mother of Jesus, draped around herself, may be a way of being touched by God.[87] Even scrapings from sacred texts of the Gospels, like the 8th-century Book of Kells in Dublin, were thought to possibly heal people when ingested.[88]

A powerful religious image that is said to have been a catalyst of healing is the painting of the crucifixion of Christ on the Isenheim altarpiece by Matthias Grunewald (1455–1528) in Germany. Painted between 1510 and 1515, this altarpiece was for St. Anthony's monastic hospital at Isenheim, with the panels showing three scenes. The first scene is the crucifixion of Christ, which is most visible, with the next, inner scene showing the dead Jesus being lowered from the cross, followed by the last scene, the resurrection. Patients at the hospital would be brought each day to sit and meditate before this crucified Jesus, dead Jesus, and then resurrected Christ, reminding them that another had suffered more than they had. An example of helping them understand that Jesus had empathy with their condition is depicted in the various scenes and biblical characters that Grunewald painted on this triptych. There were St. John the Evangelist on the left of the dying Christ, and St. John the Baptist on the right, both saints known for their intercessory powers for those with epilepsy. On the outer wings of the triptych were St. Sebastian and St. Anthony, who interceded on behalf of those who are ill.

In the perdella, the lowest section of the triptych, Jesus has his right arm cut off. Also in this scene of the dead Jesus entombed, both of his legs are amputated. This theme of amputation would help the many in the hospital who had a disease that was caused from eating moldy rye bread, leading to the amputation of one's limbs.

Grunewald's vivid depiction of the suffering of Jesus is described as follows:

> Against the pall of darkness lowered upon the earth the devastated body [of Christ] looms, dead, the flesh already discolored by decomposition and studded with the thorns of the lash. In death the strains of the superhuman agony twist the blackening feet, tear at the arms, wrench the head to one side, and turn the fingers into crooked spikes. One has only to tense his fingers in the position of Christ's to experience the shuddering tautness of nerves expressive of every line of the figure. [This is] placed in a wilderness of dark mountains, the scene is relieved by a flood of glaring light that holds the figures in a tableau of awful impact.[89]

The mood of this artwork changes radically when the panels of the altarpiece are opened, revealing the glory of Easter Sunday and the resurrection of Jesus Christ. Christ rises in a blaze of fiery light, overcoming the Roman guards; the whole scene seeming supernatural. What one can see in this scene is that our bodily cares and woes are bound only to this earth. In God's love, following one who is resurrected, the one who is currently suffering will also rise with Christ. Such good news is to have an impact upon one who is currently suffering from disease. Through such religious paintings as this by Grunewald, people were thought to be healed of their diseases or have gained new perspective on their condition: All our wounds will be taken by Christ and, in Christ, we will all be healed on the day of resurrection.

Early Residential-Care Facilities

This idea of curing and healing people by meditating on religious images carried over to religious shrines in cathedrals, where people with mental and physical impairments went in search of miraculous cures. These religious shrines existed both in Europe and outside of the Christian world. One such shrine began in the 7th century and was dedicated to Dymphna in Gheel, Belgium. According to one legend, when Dymphna's mother died, her father, the king, was obsessed with finding another woman who looked like her. But the only one who did was Dymphna herself. When the king made advances on Dymphna, which she refused, the king had her beheaded. Some of the people who were watching the execution in Gheel would have been classified as mentally ill. At the moment they saw this, as if by a miracle, they became lucid and sane.[90] To this day, Gheel has become a refuge for people with mental retardation or mental illness, where they are cared for as members of the families in whose homes they live. They are given their own bedrooms, eat meals with the families, and engage in common activities with the whole family.

Outside of Europe, there is the story of the Mansur Hospital in Cairo. In this hospital, built during the early part of the medieval period, the wards for people with disabling conditions and illnesses were cooled by fountains. There were lecture halls, a library, chapels, and a dispensary:

> There were two nurses or attendants for each resident, reciters of the Koran, musicians to lull patients to sleep; and storytellers, actors, and dancers were employed to provide diversion and distraction. Upon discharge, patients were given five gold coins to tide them over until they could find other means of support. For some reason, this model was not replicated in western Europe or other Islamic lands.[91]

By most historians' accounts, the hospital and hospice movement did its job well in the early part of the medieval ages. But the care and treatment of people with disabling conditions in these hospices varied throughout Europe. For example, in Hamburg, Germany instead of a hospice there was a tower in the middle of the city, where people with mental retardation were confined; the tower was called the "Idiot's Cage."[92] It is thought that many people who today would be labeled and classified as being "borderline mentally retarded" probably stayed at home, were seen as slow at learning certain tasks, but toiled next to the other family members. With the invention of the printing press by Johannes Gutenburg in 1457, there was a radical alteration made in Western intellectual history. The printing press led toward the development of a more literate society. With literacy came a new way of measuring intelligence, by how well one read or comprehended new material. It is possible that many people who are labeled "learning disabled" or "mentally retarded" today, diagnosed through contemporary testing services that focus on the communication of information through primarily linguistic means, would have gone undetected prior to the presence of the printing press. Most likely, they would continue to be an active part of family and church life, working out in the fields or following along in some craft.[93]

People with Disabilities During the Protestant Reformation

With the advent of the Protestant reform movement in Europe during the 15th and 16th century, and the increasing secularization of services, the hospital and hospice movement of the early Church barely survived. With the philosophical period of Enlightenment and the reformation of the Church, the plight of persons who were disabled may have reached one of its lowest periods. There was a drastic change in the power of the Roman Catholic Church throughout Europe, with new thoughts and ideas challenging the traditional, long-accepted ways of living for many people. Some of the new thoughts were as follows:

First, Paul Tillich writes that this period deserves the title "The Age of Anxiety." The anxiety of condemnation symbolized as the "wrath of God" was intensified by the imagery of hell and purgatory, driving people of the late Middle Ages to try various means of assuaging their anxiety: pilgrimages to holy places, if possible to Rome; devotion to relics; and the need for masses and penance. The ceaseless drive was found in the question: "How can I appease the wrath of God?" Death and the devil were allied in the anxious imagination of the period. Fate appears as an element within the all-embracing anxiety of guilt and in the permanent awareness of the threat of condemnation.[94]

Second, the Reformation emphasized personal responsibility, and those who could not take total responsibility for themselves were persecuted and oppressed.[95] Martin Luther embraced this doctrine in his writings. He wrote of the total depravity of men and women; we are all wholly under the power of evil and can do nothing but sin. It is Christ, and by Christ's merits alone, the Son of the One and only gracious God, that by faith, and by faith alone we are saved.[96] It is by faith in Christ that one is accounted righteous in God's sight without our cooperation.

Third, the institutions of that day were falling apart, unable to meet the basic needs of people. A series of natural calamities—crop failures, famine, pestilence, the Black Death plague, socioeconomic problems, class divisions, and corruption in the society created intense needs for health care, employment, food, shelter, and societal reform. And the Church, like other institutions, was not able to respond to all of these social needs.[97]

It was in this time of great change that reformers like Martin Luther and John Calvin brought more changes to the world and the influence of the Church universal. One of the reformers of the church, Martin Luther, influenced by the thoughts of the demonic, so prevalent in this age of anxiety, struggled with the wrath of God in the face of a 12-year-old child who was mentally retarded. In the writings called "Table Talks," or *Tishreden,* Luther's disciples wrote down his many conversations at a table where his family and friends would discuss his favorite ideas. Luther was disgusted with this 12-year-old child, saying, "he ate, defecated, and drooled." Luther recommended that he be taken to a nearby river and drowned, but his advice was not heeded:[98]

Eight years ago, there was one at Dessau whom I, Martinus Luther, saw and grappled with. He was 12 years old, had the use of his eyes and all his senses, so that one might think that he was a normal child. But he did nothing but gorge himself as much as four peasants or threshers. He ate, defecated and drooled and, if anyone tackled him, he screamed. If things didn't go well, he wept. So I said to the Prince of Anhalt: "If I were the Prince, I should take this child to the Moldau River which flows near Dessau and drown him." But the Prince of Anhalt and the Prince of Saxony, who happened to be present, refused to follow my advice. Thereupon I said: "Well, then the Christians shall order the Lord's prayer to be said in church and pray that the dear Lord take the Devil away." This was done daily in Dessau and the changeling died in the following year. When Luther was asked why he had made such a recommendation, he replied that he was firmly of the opinion that such changelings were merely a mass of flesh, a *massa carnis,* with no soul. For it is in the Devil's power that he corrupts people who have reason and souls when he possesses them. The Devil sits in such changelings where their soul should have been![99]

This theological response to a person with mental retardation was by no means unique or bizarre for that time. In 1487, the book *Malleus*

Maleficarum was published by the monks Johann Sprenger and Heinrich Kraemer. It stated that even a person with mental retardation could be considered a witch: "If the patient can be relieved by no drugs, but rather, seems to be aggravated by them, then the disease is caused by the Devil."[100]

Another leader in the Protestant reform movement was John Calvin, the French reformer and theologian, who was busy turning Geneva into a theocratic regime during this time. Like Luther, Calvin embraced the personal piety of the reformed thinking, claiming that justification was attained by faith through grace, and not by good works alone. In essence, we are no longer free creatures but are called to follow the attraction of concupiscence or God's grace.

Calvin's understanding of the nature of this relationship between God and humankind embraced the concept that God has implanted in *all* people an understanding of God's divine majesty. No nation is so barbarous, no people so savage that they do not have a deep-seated conviction that there is a God. Because all people have this conviction, no one can endure life without religion, for religion was not crafted by human beings but by God; it was ordained by God. Even those who in other respects appear to differ little from "brutes" always retain some sense of religion: "so fully are the minds of men[sic] possessed with this common principle, which is closely interwoven with their original composition."[101] Calvin wrote that some sense of the Divine God is inscribed on every heart.

This one reference to God being with even the "brutes" of this earth may be applicable to even persons with disabilities. Calvin's theology does not necessarily try to make a differentiation in how God treats persons who are disabled and non-disabled. It is possible that many authors on disabling conditions are misreading Calvin when they substitute the word "brute" for persons with disabilities. I add this because Calvin makes it clear in his writings that finally, the chief end of humanity is to worship and be in fellowship with God, as God also desires to live in our hearts.[102] Calvin's understanding of the nature of God is that of a God who is the one ground of our being. And because God is the good Creator and ground of our being, we are part of a good creation.[103]

The Rise of Residential Care

Because so many of the infrastructures of the civilian governments were in flux, and the social support systems of the Catholic and Protestant churches were so tenuous in this age of change, with monasteries being closed throughout much of Europe, the needs of persons who were disabled were not being met. There were some efforts by some Catholics to take care of babies who were abandoned because they were born unwanted or disabled. In early 18th-century Europe, one of the ways of caring for these unwanted babies was by installing a turntable in the door of foundling hospitals run by religious orders like the Vincentians, founded by St. Vincent DePaul. A baby would be placed on the turntable and passed through an opening in the door into the institution. This way, no one would need to open the door, so no one saw the parent. In 1740, there were 3,150 children left in the hands of the many Vincentian nuns and priests; in 1784 there were 40,000 children; and in 1833, there were 131,000.[104]

Outside of the Church, more private organizations, such as the craft guilds, provided for their members in times of trouble. In many ways, much of the provision of care and treatment of people with disabling conditions slowly shifted out of the hands of the religious communities and into the hands of the rising secular society.[105]

Even though the state had taken over caring for persons with disabling conditions in many ways, it did not mean that all had been well for these individuals. William Tuke, a Quaker in York, England, began a retreat center in the 1790s, York Retreat, for persons who were mentally ill. This effort came in response to the inhumane methods of the lunatic asylums of that day when a woman mysteriously died in an asylum for people with mental illnesses in York.[106] The basic methods Tuke used were "Christianity and common sense." The "common sense" involved such "radical methods" as positive reinforcement for self-control; allowing residents to wear their own clothing rather than an institutional uniform; and planning a court area for the residents to stroll in, which contained gardens and animals.[107]

Providing housing and care for people with disabilities continued into the 19th century. This idea of caring for people with disabling conditions in a segregated colony or hospital, precursor to our modern institutions, had roots in the good intentions of many Christians. For example, in 1247, the sheriff of London gave his estate and land to the bishop and church of Bethlehem to serve people with disabling conditions. In 1377, Bethlehem Hospital became what we would call an "insane asylum" when people who were either mentally retarded or mentally ill were moved there because they were too close to the king's palace. During an inventory of equipment in 1398, there were 4 pairs

of manacles, 11 chains of irons, 6 locks and keys, and 2 stocks for 20
people, while those who were less violent could roam the streets of
London, begging for food. The word "handicap" does not only pertain
to a bet on a horse; it derives from this practice of people with disabling
conditions begging on the streets for food and shelter, with their "cap-
in-hand." Soon, Bethlehem Hospital became known as "Bedlum," a
name we often associate even with our homes when things seem to
be crazy![108]

One of the more recent founders of institutional life in the field of
mental retardation was the Protestant Johann Guggenbuhl (1816–
1863), a Swiss, who had a career of extreme emotional highs and lows,
always claiming to act out of a sense of faith in God and compassion
for others. At the age of 20, Guggenbuhl observed a "dwarfed, crippled
cretin of stupid appearance" reciting the Lord's prayer in front of a
wayside cross in Switzerland. The "cretin's" mother said that she had
not been able to provide any education for him, but that he had learned
the prayer and that he went daily to pray at the cross. Guggenbuhl
wondered what could be achieved with such individuals with systematic
treatment.[109] Guggenbuhl was determined to devote his life to the
"cure and prophylaxis" of cretinism.

With this aim, he began a residential arrangement for the teaching
and the medical care of children who were mentally retarded in Abendberg, Switzerland. He proceeded to work on these cures out of the
conviction that "the immortal soul is essentially the same in every
creature born of woman." For Guggenbuhl identified himself with the
will of God: "Switzerland has indisputably been selected by Divine
Providence to shine forth before the other nations in the realization
of blissful ideas." Abendberg was one of God's merciful miracles, with
himself as the man chosen to perform them.[110]

Early America's "Christian" Response to People with Disabilities

American history, beginning with the concept of a New World in
the 16th century, has been a less-than-perfect record of care for people
with disabling conditions. In the 16th- and 17th-century witch hunts,
the civil and ecclesiastical authorities treated women and men who
would be labeled "mentally ill" as being possessed or obsessed by the

Devil.[111] The way that many were treated for their affliction was by whipping or hanging, or by the same method of "curing" people with mental retardation in the time of Luther—drowning.

But there is another side to this story. For example, people with mental retardation were first treated with a humane approach. The first governor of Massachusetts, John Winthrop, a leading Puritan leader as well, wrote in his treatise *Modell Of Christian Charity* (1630) that God has given the pilgrims in this new world a new opportunity to care for those who are less able or "regenerant":

> God Almighty in his most holy and wise providence has so disposed of the condition of mankind as at all time some must be rich, some poor, some high and eminent in power and dignity, others mean and in subjection . . . [in] the regenerant [God] exercises his graces in them, as in the great ones, their love, mercy, gentleness, temperance, and so forth in the poor and inferior sort, their faith, patience, obedience, and so forth.[112]

This spirit of caring for those who are regenerant, or mentally retarded, is carried on in the country's first code of laws as adopted by the Massachusetts General Court in December 1641:

> No man shall be pressed in person to any office, worke, warres, or other publique service, that is necessarily and suffitiently exempted by any naturall or personall impediment, as by want of yeares, greatnes of age, defect of minde, fayling of sences, or impotencie of Lymbes.
>   Children, Idiots, Distracted persons, and all that are strangers . . . shall have such allowances and dispensations in any cause whether Criminal or other as religion and reason require.[113]

In this writing for the Massachusetts court, the *Body of Liberties*, people with "defect of minde" like mental retardation and mental illness, people with "fayling of sences" like those who have visual or hearing impairments, and others with "impotencie of Lymbes", or those who are physically impaired were covered in this law as early as 1641.

The adaptation of the Elizabethan Poor Laws of 1601 also applied in the American colonies. Queen Elizabeth I issued a tax by the state to provide for the unemployable poor and to support almshouses for the aged, poor, criminals, and those who were too disabled to work.

In Rhode Island in 1647, they passed a Poor Law that saw that each town provided careful relief for the poor, "maintayned the impotent," the person with a disability.[114] But even if the state provided the funds needed in providing services to people with disabling conditions, even in the colonial period of America, the care of people with disabling conditions was the responsibility of the family. The expectation was that members of the family would provide for the needs of the person with a disabling condition, especially if they were mentally retarded.[115]

For most of the 18th and 19th centuries, both in America and in western Europe, the state provided homes, hospitals, and institutions for people with various disabling conditions in order to protect them from any harm. Families were not able to meet the changing social and economic demands at home. The state, in essence, took over as the primary caretakers for people with disabling conditions. But some of those who were institutionalized were physically, sexually, and emotionally abused.[116] It was the hope of educators and physicians alike, that, through educational means, there would be a short-term habilitation of people with disabling conditions such as mental retardation, that would later provide for easy and early reintegration back into society.

One "experiment of hope" that education would quickly habilitate people with disabling conditions faltered with the case of the Wild Boy of Aveyron, otherwise called "Victor," and his teacher, Jean Itard (1774–1838) in France. Itard was out to prove that the reason Victor was so wild was because of the lack of cognitive stimulation due to the absence of appropriate sensory experiences in his life. If Victor had a chance to have certain, keystone, sensory experiences in which the brain itself would be stimulated, then there was a chance that Victor would no longer be mentally or morally disabled. While much was learned about communicating with people orally, Itard concluded that the experience was a failure because Victor's progress was slow and difficult. When Victor could not cope with a new exercise, he would become violent.[117]

One of the students of Itard was the physician Eduoard Seguin. Seguin believed that there was a definite neurophysical relationship between sensory activity and higher levels of thinking. What eyes, ears, taste buds, touch, and nose took in influenced one's cognitive development. Seguin's methods was the "Trinitarian hypothesis":

> We shall have to educate the activity, the intelligence, the will, three functions of the unit man, not three entities antagonistic one

of the other. We shall have to educate them, not with a serial object in view, but with a sense of their unity in the one being.[118]

For the Christian religious educator, as well as special educators, it is novel to see included in educating children with mental retardation their behavioral actions, their cognitive development, and their moral will, as well as the role of Christian activities: The children with mental retardation were at morning hymns at 5:30 A.M. and evening hymns at 8:15 P.M. Essential to Itard's and Seguin's training of people with mental retardation was participation in the worship life of the Church.

This optimistic perception of habilitating people with disabling conditions, especially mental retardation, was short lived. It was later, at the turn of the century, that society realized the possibility of habilitating people with disabling conditions like mental retardation was not going to happen quickly. People with disabling conditions were joining the number of those defined as poor, some engaging in criminal activity; others merely regressed in their ability within the community. Soon, people with disabling conditions were seen as a threat toward people in society. No longer were the institutions and hospitals there to protect the people with disabling conditions: they were maintained to protect the larger public from people with disabling conditions, especially those with mental retardation and mental illnesses.[119]

Even with the deinstitutionalization model, the emergence of people with disabling conditions from these settings has neither been emotionally painless, economically free, nor easy on the family, the Church, and society. The neurologist and author Oliver Sacks wrote that deinstitutionalization has not worked because of the lack of a communal sense of responsibility. People with disabling conditions like mental illness and mental retardation have "rapidly drifted into homelessness, destitution, misery, and sometimes death."[120] It is from this very world view that people with various disabling conditions are still fighting to get out, seeking some voice and visible presence in a world that has long been deaf and blind to the cries and protests of people with disabling conditions, who wish nothing more than to be included and accepted as invaluable members not only of society, but more importantly, of our churches.

A Response of the Church to Theodicy

One major lesson that we may draw from this historic overview is that the presence of people with disabilities is not new to the world in general, or to churches in particular. Nor have our very human society, or more specifically, our parishes and congregations, really changed in the way they perceive work, live, and interact with those labeled "impaired." The Church is still struggling with the mere acceptance of people with disabling conditions, let alone working on the task of worshiping, living, and learning from them. As we see through this historical sketch, people with disabling conditions have been living and working, struggling and hurting, in the midst of the larger able-bodied society since the beginning of time.

Another major lesson from this brief historical overview is the knowledge that throughout human history, people have been seen as having disabling conditions because of something they have brought upon themselves, or because of an act of God, or because of the unholy mischief of Satan. Regardless of the cause or causes of the disabling condition, there is often great dis-ease among people who are able bodied when they are in the company of someone who is disabled. Those who are able bodied are uncomfortable enough with the severe limitations or different ways of being in the world that we question God, or search for medical, therapeutic, or educational answers, if not for a miraculous cure to heal the other person, making him or her just like us. This is why the early Church built hospices. This is why people continue to go on pilgrimages and meditate on religious objects and images. This is why there were drownings of people with disabling conditions. This is why we continue to set aside the person with a disability in a unit at a psychiatric hospital, geographically and mentally removed from the rest of society. The "normal" community is just uncomfortable, in a constant state of unrest among those with disabling conditions. We're so uncomfortable with what someone cannot do that we fail to appreciate who the person is.

Theologically, assuming that the person with a disability is suffering or hurting from being disabled, the conventional theodicy question that is often asked within the Church is as follows:

> If God is loving and at the same time all-powerful, then why is there so much suffering in the world? The assumption is that the deity *could* if the deity *would*, simply eliminate suffering.[121]

Rabbi Harold Kushner asked this same question in his book *When Bad Things Happen To Good People* in which the title makes some bold assumptions about what is bad (a disabling condition), who is "good" (people who worship God), and the very nature of God's power and love (limited omnipotence).

But the theodicy question cannot be adequately addressed, for it pits God's love against God's power. The theologian Stanley Hauerwas writes that the very problem with theodicy is that it is rooted in the philosophical ideals of the Enlightenment. In the Enlightenment, people became proud of their intellects and the ability of human beings to think rationally and logically. People in this "Age of Reason" valued intellectual religion and propositional statements about truth. One of the consequences was that the Church became "more like a lecture hall, and the pastor a mere lecturer on doctrine and morality. The Church suffered from this mistaken notion that religion is true and of value to the extent to which it can be intellectually intelligible."[122]

In the Enlightenment world view, God became a creation of human imagination. God's existence could be shown, proven, or known by philosophical means.[123] Philosophers of the Enlightenment supported extending human power over all contingencies in life, including suffering: "If god cannot eliminate suffering, even though god may have the power to do so, then we will have to do god's task to insure that god can remain god."[124] The problem of evil in the theodical world view of the Enlightenment is that the modern world's idea of evil is like their creation of a God: Both could be known outside and separated from a community of people at worship, like the Church.[125]

What is interesting is that the problem of evil and suffering did not have to be explained or rationalized. Hauerwas writes that it was important *not* to give a theoretical account of why such evil needed to be in order that certain good results occur, "since such an explanation would undercut the necessity of the community capable of absorbing the suffering."[126] Hauerwas then quotes the scholar Kenneth Surin:

> The "problem of evil" arises (at least in part) when *particular* narratives of events of pain, dereliction, anguish, oppression, torture, humiliation, degradation, injustice, hunger, godforsakenness, and so on, come into collision with the Christian community's narratives, which are inextricably bound up with the redeeming reality of the triune God.[127]

Hauerwas rightly argues that, for Christians, suffering cannot be separated from their calling to be a new people made holy by conversion, which is inseparable from the body or community, or the Banquet Feast, of Christians in unity with the Holy Trinity.[128] Suffering and evil, therefore, becomes a practical challenge, not a problem, for the Christian community as a whole.

The Christian community does not have a "solution" to the problem of evil or to the nature of suffering. Instead, because the Christian community is located in God's unfolding sacred narrative—the God who has not abandoned us even when we felt deeply ill—those people with any kind of disabling conditions have had a community of care that has made it possible for them to absorb the destructive terror of evil that constantly threatens to destroy all human relationships.[129]

In conclusion, what we know from this historical sketch is that people will always have some kind of disabling condition, limitation, or shortcoming of one kind or another. It is part and parcel of the human condition. Yet people rarely "suffer" from having a disability like a sensory impairment, a developmental disability, or physical impairment, unless they are physically ill. What they are suffering from is the harshness of the world around them, and the cruelty and oppression in the continual assault found in the great effort to transform everyone who is different to be *"just like me,"* rather than more like themselves—the person that God created them to be. Perhaps what needs to be "cured" here is not disabling conditions but our perception and subsequent reaction to people whom society has labeled as impaired. Instead of looking at how impossible it is for people who are able bodied and those who are disabled to relate to and live with each other because of our differences, maybe what we need to start considering is what we have in common as well as what makes us strangers to one another.

The inclusion of people with disabling conditions is essential in congregations and parishes because they are children of God and children of the Church, whom the Church would not choose to be without. People with disabling conditions challenge and excite our collective imagination in the multitude of ways that we may be a more caring, compassionate community of Christians.

Stanley Hauerwas rightly understands the necessity of people with disabilities in our congregations and parishes because they challenge our presuppositions about community, as well as the nature of God. As for the Christian community, people with disabilities challenge the limitations of our practices. We learn to rediscover the beauty of Holy

Scripture through sign language; we learn to take our time walking to a pew as the usher is in a wheelchair; we learn to relinquish ourselves to God in worship by joining in the hand signs of the child with autistic behavior.

In terms of our knowing God, people with disabilities like mental retardation or autism create a "wildness" that frightens us because they are not easily domesticated:

> Yet exactly to the extent that they create the unexpected they remind us that the God we worship is not easily domesticated. For in worship the church is made vulnerable to a God that would rule this world not by coercion but through the unpredictability of love.[130]

And so the Christian community invites those people whom society has labeled "disabled," to God's Banquet Feast on earth, the Church, precisely because they are the ones who disturb us. In their disturbance, God brings a gift through the unexpected guest.[131] The gift is one of gentle humility. For example, consider Jesus' parable of someone who was invited to a wedding banquet: Jesus told him not to sit down at the place of honor, but to go and sit down at the lowest place, so that when the host comes, he may say "Friend, move up higher; then you will be honored in the presence of all who sit at the table with you" (Luke 14:13, NRSV).

Those with disabilities bring the gifts of insecurity and of dependence on and attentiveness toward God. Even though there is something within us that desires independence from God, to be secure in our own ways—traits that were apparent in the Genesis account of creation—God expects us to welcome strangers, for they help the Church become a network of relationships of truth. They help bring an openness to God and to others necessary for us to be the Church of Jesus Christ.

The lesson learned is that we are all brothers and sisters in Christ, regardless of our abilities or limitations. Learning to be with those with disabling conditions also provides them an opportunity to be with us. And together, we become a community, for a community is a place of belonging, where all people discover whose they are: We are all God's beloved.

4

Welcoming the Unexpected Guests to the Banquet

In her book *The Rituals of Dinner*, Margaret Visser accurately points out the social importance of dining together, turning the consumption of food, a biological necessity, into a carefully cultured phenomenon:

> We use eating as a medium for social relationships: satisfaction of the most individual of needs becomes a means of creation community. [132]

The truth of this statement became reality for me when I was living in a l'Arche community, the Christian communities for people with mental retardation that Jean Vanier founded, where a wonderfully strange assortment of individuals became a living community during dinner.

Some of the most memorable parts of living and working in both British and American l'Arche communities came during the evening meals. Gathered around a large wooden table are all the members of a l'Arche household and, on most evenings, a guest or stranger or two. In some houses, the guest's place is marked by a decorated paper napkin. At dinnertime, all the folks who live in the house come together to eat the meal prepared jointly by a team of assistants, the careworkers in a l'Arche community, and the core members of l'Arche, those who are mentally retarded. They also come to engage in conversation, to become a community again. The gathering sometimes gets quite noisy and rambunctious, laughter-filled, and quarrelsome, with food passing all around the table, stopping only briefly for the singing of an opening prayer to God. All members are interested in finding out the basics: What happened to *you* today in the workshop, in the office, or at home? All participate in some measure in the discussion, each having their basic need for food met as well as their basic need for relationships, being with one another.

The meal may last anywhere from 30 to 90 minutes. It is more than coming together just to eat, but an occasion to check in with one another and find out how the other person is, a break in the busyness of the day. Once the opening prayer is over, food is served, "family style," with one or two people serving the rest of the household of 6, up to maybe 16 people.

At one evening meal in a house in the Lambeth l'Arche community in London, England, I remember the wonderful banter among people while the plates were quickly being passed around the table, water poured in tea mugs, with no one missing a beat. George, who is mentally retarded, said how much he had been "suffering" because the hot water heater had been broken in his house. George is tired of cold baths! Cliff, the newest member of the household, who is mentally retarded, excitedly talked about his plans for going home to visit his parents for the first time since he moved into the house four weeks ago. During this conversation, Sue, a woman who is disabled, would calmly pat my arm, and, with a mouth full of food say "Ah, aren't you lovely!"

The assistants also try to have a conversation with one another; those working in the house wanted to find out what happened to those working in the workshop. There are moments of great gales of laughter as assistants have napkins and napkin rings "stolen" from their places, to miraculously reappear in the hands of someone else at the opposite end of the table.

At the end of the meal, after the dinner plates have been taken away, the tea has been poured, and fruit or dessert has been eaten, there is a moment for reflection. A single candle may be lit and placed in the center of the gathering circled around the table, and the lights dimmed. Scripture is read, maybe accompanied by a story pertaining to the Scripture reading, and prayers quietly begin. Matthew, who has cerebral palsy, begins with thanking God for his "Mum, Dad, and *our* house!" Beatrice prays to God that she be less stubborn among and with other people. Both Matthew's and Beatrice's prayers are hard to understand because of their own speech limitations, but after a few conversations with them, one slowly develops an ear for their speech pattern and can clearly understand what it is that they are telling God in their prayers.

Lydia, an assistant, prays for the many l'Arche communities around the world. Ben, another assistant, prays for his aunt who is ill at home. A moment after the prayers are over, a song, common to all the l'Arche communities in Britain, is sung. At the conclusion of the song, the meal over, the lights come back up, plates are taken out to be washed by hand by all who did not cook the meal, a time known by some as "the spirituality of the sink," while others go on with evening activities. [133]

In some sense, the physical needs of the body and the needs of the human spirit are fed at this one table as *all* the members gather together to be and become a living community. Jean Vanier writes that such evening meals are a daily celebration of a community's life, where we meet each other and share in the joy and struggle of each other's life and the life of Christ. It is a delight for both the stomach and the bodily senses, as well as a delight of friendship and love, which makes the whole activity human. [134] At the heart of a l'Arche community is celebration, a concrete and tangible way of living and rejoicing in life together. Celebration is a specific act of a community—"it is a cry to covenant together." [135]

What does an evening meal in a l'Arche house have to do with a book on Christian ministry with people with disabilities? Everything! For this evening meal in a l'Arche community may be a fitting metaphor for guiding congregations and parishes towards being more of an inclusive gathering. Like the evening meal in the l'Arche house, churches should have plenty of room for friends and unexpected strangers; they should be eager to find a place for all to sit and participate. As in this evening meal, there is always plenty of physical and spiritual food for those who are hungry within God's house. Like the l'Arche house, the congregation or parish reminds the participants of our common reliance on one another for what we do and who we are in life, and of our common dependency on the love of God. At the table, as in other communities of faith, the members come together and share their unique stories of life and their shared dependence upon one another and God: In essence, they are living the life of community.

In the preceding chapters, the problems that congregations and the community of people with disabilities face in integrating Christ's community have been discussed. Throughout these chapters there have been hints and suggestions concerning our problematic perception of people with disabilities and their absence from active congregational participation. A way of undoing the surmountable problems and reenvisioning the crisis situation has been offered with the suggestive use of Jesus' metaphor of the Banquet Feast. This chapter's focus is on the great symbolic or metaphorical meaning of the Great Banquet Feast for the Church that is serious about not only learning *how* to welcome those with disabilities, but *why* the inclusion of people with disabilities is essential for the Church to be the Church of Jesus Christ. For it is only when we learn how to be with those who are different from us, and learn to accept the love of God that we all need, that we will be able to sustain a community that is capable of worshiping God.[136]

This next section will briefly identify the current scarcity paradigm that many churches have been operating from, which explains why many congregations and parishes just don't believe they can afford to welcome and meet the complex needs and concerns of people with disabilities. A response to this scarcity paradigm is made by focusing on a paradigm of abundance, as is described in Jesus' parable of the Great Banquet Feast; a paradigm that will challenge the collective imagination of our congregations and churches in beginning and continuing the work of inviting, welcoming, and accepting people with disabilities into the worshiping community of Christians.

Scarcity in the Church

In each of the preceding chapters, there have been stories of people with disabilities and their families who have not felt invited, welcomed, or accepted into the life of a congregation or parish. Instead, they have felt uninvited, misunderstood, patronized, and ignored by the community of Christ. They have been set on the margins of the Church because the Church does not know what else to do with them. In doing so, the community is no longer composed of people with all their richness, weakness, and poverty; of people who accept and forgive each other; people who are vulnerable to one another and to God.[137]

Their simple need and strong desire to worship God remains unheard and ignored, and they have no other community to turn to and nowhere else to belong.

Why do many congregations and parishes respond in this way? Is it because these communities are only for perfect people with no problems? Many congregations and parishes understand community life from what some anthropologists describe as a scarcity paradigm. The anthropologist Richard Katz wrote that the scarcity paradigm assumes that certain valued resources are scarce. Such scarce resources can include items from oil and water, to health care and help for people with disabling conditions. Some even perceive of love as a scarce resource, fearful that they may squander it in the wrong places, using it all with none left in reserve for an emergency. They are not aware that this is backward thinking; in reality, the more we share love with one another, the more we have of it. The scarcity paradigm is a justified description of our contemporary American culture, and from such cultural pressures none of us are exempt, including those of us who consider themselves members of Christ's body. Life becomes a struggle to accumulate our own supply of goods, and to resist pressures to share what we have with others.[138]

In other ways, churches have also worked out of this scarcity paradigm when discussing ways of caring for and working with people who are disabled. Four characteristics of this scarcity paradigm related to the issue of integrating people with disabilities into the Church are as follows:

First, valued resources, including health services and helping, are neither renewable nor expendable. Good health care and adaptive services for people with disabling conditions in churches cost money, time, and energy.

For example, in some congregations there may be only a limited number of large-print Bibles so that not everyone who is visually impaired will be able to have one. Or someone who is severely or profoundly mentally retarded may want to be included in the life of a youth group, but the gathering is too small, and there is no one trained in special education to help: "Sorry, but no one with a disabling condition can come this Sunday." This assumes, of course, that special training is necessary.

In other cases, many people have not been confirmed into the life of a church because there hasn't been anyone to communicate with a person with an impairment what is happening in worship, religious education activities, or youth groups.

Second, many financially wealthy congregations or parishes who do have the resources to make their places of worship inclusive and accessible to people with various disabling conditions simply do not choose to do so. In many cases, only the larger, financially well-endowed parishes and congregations can afford to have wheelchair ramps or to hire someone to sign the sermon for people with hearing impairments. Many churches cannot afford to build a ramp onto a building, or to pay a person to work with someone who is hearing impaired, or to type the sermon into braille, or to help a young person in youth group participate in an outing.

Third, what is good for one is not necessarily seen as good for all in the life of the Church. Concerning worship, I have heard more than once that the reason people with some disabling conditions, such as profound mental retardation, autism, mental illness, or cerebral palsy that effects one's speech, are not included in worship is because their presence will interrupt the service for those who are trying to enjoy the quiet, orderly worship. This excuse has been used not only for people with disabling conditions but also for children in worship.

Some parishes have a "chapel of tears" or "weeping chapels" where parents with crying infants and people with disabling conditions are encouraged to go during worship and can make as much noise as they want. There is usually an intercom system so that those who are there can still hear what is happening outside, but cannot necessarily participate with the other members of the worshipping community. This assumes that the place of worship is a place for only those who are quiet in the worship of God.

Fourth, the whole is not greater than the sum of the parts after all. There has been a fragmentation, making inclusion of people with disabling conditions a cause that is not quite as important as are issues concerning racism, classism, and sexism.

For example, consider a course in liberation theology that I took as a seminarian. When I raised the issue of "handicapism" to one of the professors, she said she knew little in the area, and that we had enough to do with racism, classism, and sexism in the church. Thus went another opportunity to awaken the leaders-to-be of congregations and parishes to an important cause.

Overall, in using this scarcity paradigm as a framework for interpreting the actions of some churches in response to including people with disabling conditions, it is easier to understand why some people with disabling conditions have been locked out, segregated, closed off, and set on the margins of our Christian communities. Many parishes and congregations have been operating out of a scarcity paradigm that suggests that we live in a world of scarce and finite resources. With this model in place, our work with people who are disabled has been largely that of isolating those with a condition away from the rest of us, sequestering them into programs with specialists who alone can deal with their "problems."

What is interesting is that while congregations still work from a segregated model for the inclusion of many people with disabling conditions, public places like schools are required by the federal and state laws to place children with disabling conditions into "the least restrictive environment" and "mainstreamed" programs in the regular schools. And with the recent passage of the Americans with Disabilities Act (ADA), individuals with disabilities who are qualified for employment or promotion will not have them denied simply because of their disabilities.[139]

However, there are still forces working in our society that argue for the segregation of people with disabling conditions from the rest of "normal" society. This goes from including segregated time in separated classes for children with disabilities, to "hospitals" where children with emotional and behavioral disabilities might be "cured." In many neighborhoods in America there are segregated group homes for adults with mental illness or mental retardation struggling for acceptance. The segregationist forces are still at work in the larger society, and it is this world view that has influenced the practices within churches.

Having identified and criticized the scarcity paradigm, which may help explain why people with disabling conditions have been kept out of our churches, it is important to search for creative and constructive alternative approaches or models for congregations and parishes. The hope is to find a model that will enable churches to be all embracing and all inclusive, where all may worship and play, sing and dance, reflect and celebrate the Word of God.

What is needed is a metaphor or paradigm that will make it possible for the congregations and parishes to not only hear but act according to the life of Jesus. The theologian Sallie McFague suggests that one of the most powerful ways for the Church to hear and receive the

Good News is by attending to Jesus' parables as models of theological reflection, for the parables remind us of the life we are called to by God.[140] Jesus told parables to people in hopes that these stories of common people in common places would enable his followers to better understand God and God's kingdom, like the parable of the Great Banquet.

Parables and the Kingdom of God

Along with the parable of the Banquet Feast as an extended metaphor for the Kingdom of God, Jesus described God's Kingdom using other innovative metaphors and analogies. For example, the Kingdom is compared to a mustard seed (Luke 13:18–19); the invaluable nature of the Kingdom is described in the parable of the hidden talents (Matthew 25:14–20); and the paradoxical complexity of entering the Kingdom if one is rich is compared to the difficulty of a camel passing through the eye of a needle (Luke 18:18–25).

In the New Testament, Jesus taught those who followed him about the Kingdom of God, emphasizing what it had meant to his ancestors before him: that God's Kingdom will bring all of creation to a sense of wholeness and completion.[141] At the heart of Jesus' ministry was the task of preaching and teaching about the good news: that the Kingdom of God is at hand, an idea that is reinforced in the Lord's Prayer (Matt. 6:9–10):

> Our Father in heaven, hallowed be your name. Your kingdom come, your will be done, on earth as it is in heaven.

For the Christian community, such parables and prayers of God's Kingdom are crucial, for the goal of what the Church aims for and points to is the kingdom of God. The theologian Lesslie Newbigin talks of these messages about God's Kingdom as being presented to a community in which the foretaste of the Kingdom already exists. The kingdom of God calls people to be part of God's holy community, an invitation that all Christians are given not because of anything they have done but simply because they are called.[142]

It is important to remember in this discussion of the Kingdom of God that the Church is *not* the Kingdom of God. The biblical scholar Marcus Borg writes that the Kingdom is something to be hoped for, something to be brought about by the power of God.[143] The images of the Kingdom of God that Jesus shared with his followers serve as the penultimate goal of the Church; the members of a church are called by Jesus to strive for God's Kingdom (Luke 12:31, NRSV).

In striving for the Kingdom of God, placing its very collective life into God's unfolding story, the Church depends on these graphic stories and creative images that Jesus Christ used in his parables. God's love is never abstract. It does not adhere to the abstract in theoretical and theological formulas, but to the lilies of the field, the sparrows in the barn, to the least of these among my brothers and sisters.[144] The images that Jesus used for the Kingdom of God continue to serve the Church well as they present a vital, concrete picture of where it is in relationship to "the communion of saints."[145]

For this book, the image of the Kingdom of God for congregations and parishes is that of the Banquet Table (Luke 14:15–26). This image of the Kingdom reveals the manner in which people come to God's gathering, through the Host's gracious invitation. The Banquet Table demonstrates how important the spirit of welcome and hospitality is in greeting all those who gather around God's feast. The image of the Banquet Table also conveys the spirit of acceptance, for one's identity is found only at God's love feast. It is at the Banquet Table of God that all people find their place.

Banquets in Luke 14

The title of this chapter, "Welcoming the Unexpected Guests to the Banquet" finds its inspiration from the story that Jesus told about the Great Banquet in Luke 14:15–24. This story was chosen because it is an uplifting one where people with disabilities, considered lowly in Jewish society, were transformed into the invited guests as a banquet meal arranged by a most powerful yet gracious host. In this parable, the reader begins to see a glimmer of hope where before only dark despair appeared; normality where there was only a sense of wild abnormality; and cosmos where there was only chaos.

This parable of the Banquet Feast, along with the other stories from Luke 14, are especially poignant for this issue as Jesus reveals something important about the very nature of the kingdom of God. What occurs in the stories in this chapter is a reversal of roles, where those who are poor, and those with disabling conditions, like the "crippled, blind and lame," are not the outsiders to God's kingdom (Luke 14:2, 13, and 21, NRSV). The presence of people with disabilities in these stories sheds light on how inclusive the Kingdom of God is in welcoming and accepting those who are disabled as God's chosen.

In the Gospel of Luke, Jesus is often referred to as "the Son of Man," God now one with humankind, addressing the concerns of those who are poor, robbed of the material possessions others have. Jesus is actively concerned with the plight of those who are poor and "unfortunate" in the ways of the world, like those who are disabled.[146]

Jesus' care and concern for those who are outcasts of society, such as those with disabling conditions, is well demonstrated in three stories found in Luke 14. As one commentary writer points out, the three stories are held together by the central motif of the banqueting table: verse 1 is about entering into a room where the feast is about to happen; verse 7 is about choosing a place to sit and eat; verse 12 has to do with lunch or dinner; and verse 16 concerns those gathered around the banqueting table.[147] In each of these stories, a person, or persons, with some disabling condition is central to revealing something new about the Kingdom of God that Jesus has been talking about and proclaiming to his disciples, the crowds, and even the Pharisees.

The first two stories found in Luke that bring Jesus together with the Pharisees and people with disabling conditions are as follows:

Luke 14:1–6: Pronouncement

This is a "pronouncement story," where Jesus uses this situation to reveal that, being one with God, he has the authority to heal a man with "dropsy," or edema, even on the Sabbath.[148] The scandal in this occasion is that in healing the man he breaks the Law of Moses and Talmudic laws of "working" rather than resting on the Sabbath.

When Jesus went to the house of a Pharisee to eat a meal on the Sabbath, he cured a person with dropsy. With Jesus at his polemical best, he asks those who tell him that he cannot heal on the Sabbath, "If one of you has a child or an ox that has fallen into a well, will you not immediately pull it out on a sabbath day?" In other words, the life of this person, even this outcast with the disabling condition of dropsy, is far more important than living strictly to the letter of the Law. The response of the audience is silence, which, as some commentaries report, means that the Pharisees and lawyers agreed with what Jesus said: "They could not reply to this" (verse 6).[149]

Luke 14:7–15: Table Manners

This story involves table manners for the Kingdom of God. Jesus makes it clear to the listeners that there is a code of conduct to be followed in our relationship with others, especially those who are "poor, crippled, lame and blind" (verse 13).

In this next scene, Jesus notices where the guests and host sit at the table for the upcoming meal. He tells them a parable: "When you are invited by someone to a wedding banquet, do not sit down at the place of honor." He goes on to say that real honor among people, and in the presence of God, does not come from self-seeking choices, from always being invited to sit in places of honor. Instead, the position Jesus encourages the listening crowd to take is to sit in the lowlier places around the table, inviting those who cannot repay you with such a luxurious meal, like the "poor, the crippled, the lame, and the blind," to sit in the places of honor (verse 13). One's final reward will be repaid at "the resurrection of the righteous" (verse 14). In other words, the host's recompense will not come from those who are less fortunate—from those who are disabled and will probably never be able to supply a similar cordiality—but from God in the latter days.

It is clear that Jesus is not teaching the rules of "proper etiquette" in these stories, but making the point that God alone will invite those God wants to the banquet of life, with those who are considered "the least" in Jewish society sitting closer to the head of the table.[150] Those who are disabled and come to the meal will never be able to have such a lavish house, nor host such an impressive gathering, because they are the poorest in Jewish society, left to begging on street corners. The host is therefore seen as making a most humble gesture of feeding those who can never repay this gracious, generous act of love.

What is important to note in both of these stories is that those who are disabled or crippled (which in New Testament Greek is *anapeirous*, meaning "lame and blind") are used by Jesus as the agents of change: Their very presence in these stories reveals something about God's reign.[151] In the first story, healing the person with dropsy, caring for another human being, even on Sabbath, may mean that God in Christ truly cares more for our very being than for our religious following of the Law only. In the second story, the inclusion of people with disabling conditions reveals that God truly cares for those who are unfortunate.

Luke 14:15–24: The Parable of the Great Banquet

In this parable of the Great Banquet in Luke 14:15–24, there is a story about people's reaction to the invitation to share in the Messianic feast that becomes a model for the Kingdom of God, a banquet feast prepared and hosted by God. It is also a parable that describes how God will provide for all those invited, especially the outcasts of Jewish society—those who are disabled.[152]

It is helpful to know that any banquet feast is an exceptional occasion, an extravagance of great richness, given as a celebration of relationships among the diners, and also as an expression of order, knowledge, competencies, sympathy, and consensus about the important aspects of living. The intended goal of a banquet is that the food and company will recall the happiness of memories from an earlier time.[153] In capturing the memories of things past, the banquet reminds the participants of a triple alliance: It links people to God; it causes them to remember their place in the natural world; and it reinforces our social interdependence with others.[154]

In this case, the parable of the Banquet Feast is an idea that Jesus borrows from his Jewish heritage. Among those in the Jewish community, the metaphor of the banqueting table refers to the past leaders of the children of Israel, gathered together around the special religious Messianic banquet. At that time, Abraham, Isaac, and Jacob, and all the prophets, will come together with all the children of Israel, with Yahweh as the host.[155] As such, the banquet feast was, and still is, a reflection of God's cosmos, an omnipresent order.[156]

The Great Banquet parable is symbolic of an inclusive congregation, otherwise known as a "Kingdom Parable," presenting to us some new characteristics about the Kingdom of God:[157]

> One of the dinner guests, on hearing this, said to him, "Blessed is the one who will eat bread in the kingdom of God!" Then Jesus said to him, "Someone gave a great dinner and invited many. At the time for the dinner he sent his slave to say to those who had been invited, 'Come; for everything is ready now.' But they all alike began to make excuses. The first said to him, 'I have bought a piece of land, and I must go out and see it; please accept my

regrets.' Another said, 'I have bought five yoke of oxen, and I am going to try them out; please accept my regrets.' Another said, 'I have just been married, and therefore I cannot come.' So the slave returned and reported this to his master. Then the owner of the house became angry and said to his slave, 'Go out at once into the streets and lanes of the town and bring in the poor, the crippled, the blind, and the lame.' And the slave said, 'Sir, what you ordered has been done, and there is still room.' Then the master said to the slave, 'Go out into the roads and lanes, and compel people to come in, so that my house may be filled. For I tell you, none of those who were invited will taste my dinner'" (Luke 14:15–24, NRSV).

Jesus' parable presents to those receiving the story an idea about the inclusive nature of the kingdom of God. New Testament commentary writers and theologians agree that the host of this banquet, the grand host of the feast, is God.[158] As at any other banquet meal, the host is in a powerful position, able to persuade people to come and remain a part of a scene. If a banquet is a stage performance, then the host has the right to choose the right cast (or the right guests), or else the dinner performance is a failure.[159]

Metaphorically, the servant in this story is Jesus. The guests also serve an important role, for there can be no festive banquet without them. They are needed to show support, and to renew neighborly bonds with the host.[160] Those who come from the "streets and lanes of the town" suggest the people of the rural land; the "roads and lanes" are the largely Gentile world; and "the poor, the crippled, the blind, and the lame" are the largely godless, largely outcast world whom God turns to and calls to be part of the Kingdom.[161]

In this story, the host has invited three prominent men, and probably their families, to come to a large banquet he has prepared, but they have all refused him; they are all too busy with their own mundane lives to take time to accept the gracious invitation of the host to this elaborate feast. As is required by ancient Near East etiquette, they are extended a second invitation, which they refuse yet again: One because he had just bought land that he wanted to see; another because he had just bought a cow he wanted to see; and the third because he had just been married and he wanted time with his family. All three men are consumed and controlled by what, in the presence of God, appear to be the trivial and mundane tasks of everyday life. They have no time to take off to be at this banquet feast. This was seen in Jewish society as a serious breach of friendship.[162] The three invited friends needed to remember that they are members of a greater family and of the household of God. They struggle with the good things of this life, namely property, occupation, and family, that often crowd out the claims of God upon their lives.

The host, angry at this response of the three invited friends, sends his servant out to do something unheard of: "Go out at once into the streets and lanes of the town and bring in the poor, those who are disabled, those who are visually impaired, and those who are physically impaired" (verse 21). The outcasts, those people from the leper colonies, those who sit at the city gates and beg for money to buy bread, those who steal from others along the highways and the dark alley ways to survive and support themselves, those who have no hope for their own welfare in Jewish society—the true outcasts are the ones who are finally invited to come. At first, they stall because they do not feel worthy and decline the invitation. But they are reassured and gently taken into the house.[163]

In the last verse of this story, the host is telling the servant the theological point of the story: "None of those who were invited will taste my dinner" (verse 24). None of those who were first invited— the ones that the host, God, first desired to entertain and welcome— will now be included. They, not God the host, excluded themselves from the banquet. Instead, those empty places will be filled by those seen as the most unlikely participants in this grand banquet. God in Christ takes those with disabilities who have been rejected by the rest of Jewish society, a microcosmic reflection of the rest of humanity, and transforms them from outcasts to honorably invited guests to the banquet of love, the kingdom of God.

Who do the people who are poor and those who are disabled symbolically represent in this story? All of us. Those who are disabled also represent us. They represent all of us who come before God to sit at a table of love and life with one another and share in a meal, with all our wounds and sense of brokenness, with all our limitations and knowledge of our inadequacies, with all our sins well known already by God we come to share in the banquet presented before us. The invitation is not determined by a person's good works or good actions, but by accepting the simple invitation God has extended out of love for his children.

But this story also makes it clear that without God's invitation, you cannot come to the banquet or even sit at the table. No one can remain outside of the kingdom of God but by one's own choice; we can only exclude ourselves from this gathering.[164] There is no stand-by or waiting line at this table: The parable reveals that our place at the feast is determined not by our human deeds but by God's gracious, loving invitation to come and sup at the banquet table ("Come, for everything is ready now," says the master, God, to the servant Jesus [verse 17]). If we do not come, it is because of our preoccupation with the things of this world, not because God has not invited us.

Lessons Learned From God's Banquet Feast

There are many lessons to be learned from this parable as we are challenged to use our imagination in envisioning what such a feast would look, sound, smell, feel, and taste like once the unexpected guests actually come to God's Banquet Feast. The Presbyterian minister-writer Frederick Buechner describes this colorful gathering as follows:

> The string ensemble strikes up the overture to "The Bartered Bride," the champagne glasses are filled, the cold pheasant is passed round, and there they sit by candlelight with their white canes and their empty sleeves, their Youngstown haircuts, their orthopedic shoes, their sleazy clothes, their aluminum walkers. A woman with a harelip proposes a toast. An old man with the face of Lear on the heath and a party hat does his best to rise to his feet. A deaf-mute thinks people are starting to go home and pushes back from the table. Rose petals float in the finger bowls. The strings shift into the Liebestod.[165]

This is a humorous yet poignant lesson that Buechner garnered from this parable. It implies for us readers and listeners that the banquet table of God is peopled by the most unlikely characters we could ever have imagined. Those who populate this table are the unexpected ones, the people that most of us would never consider inviting to our homes, unless you are part of a community like a l'Arche gathering. At the banqueting table are the unexpected guests of God. Yet this is one of the points of the parable: One's presence in the Kingdom of

God is not determined by what we do or how we look to others. One's presence at this grand banquet is determined by whom God invites, and who kindly and graciously accepts the invitation. It is, in the end, all dependent upon God. It is God's banqueting feast, God's Kingdom, that we—all of us, no matter what our abilities or limitations may be—are called to come and be part of. Drop everything you are doing, for all is now ready.

Another possible interpretation may resemble "The Dinner Party," begun in 1974 by the artist Judy Chicago and now exhibited at the Brooklyn Museum of Art in New York. This dinner party table consists of an equilateral triangle 48 feet per side with 39 place settings, a marble floor underneath with 999 names inscribed, all celebrating and commemorating women in history and legend. Each place setting includes a ceramic plate, with a central raised motif designed by the artist to symbolize the woman honored, along with a runner reflecting the subject's period, and a cup. The purpose of this artistic masterpiece is to celebrate the rich heritage of all women, affirming their presence in our world.[166]

In a sense, the banquet table of Jesus' parable also celebrates and affirms the presence and the importance of all people, especially those who are labeled by society as disabled. Imagine at this common banquet table that God the Host has put a place card, announcing who is sitting there, with a unique plate, cup, and runner that reflects that person's story. This is what the parable does: It points out that in the Kingdom of God those whom society sees as the outcasts—the "disabled ones"—are truly the wisest ones who kindly and graciously accept the invitation to be part of God's Kingdom.

No matter which interpretation one selects, this is a powerful parable that may truly influence our ecclesiological imagination, encouraging us to find ways to welcome people with disabling conditions in light of God's invitation to include those labeled as "disabled" by society. It will also, in pragmatic terms, help us in reflecting on the very configuration of our congregation and parishes. If our parishes and congregations are communities that are sustained by the stories we find in the Bible, revealing God's love and the nature of God's Kingdom, including those who are seen by others as disabled, and we, as members of this gathering, are "members one of another" (Ephesians 4:25), then we have a basis for common action so that our ordinary lives in the community of Christian faith more closely reflect our shared vision of

God's Kingdom.[167] Stanley Hauerwas writes that these stories, and subsequent interpretation of these stories, may provide some sense that we are all more like one another than unlike one another.[168]

Using some of the stories I have heard and experiences collected, observations from living in l'Arche communities, and work with churches in welcoming people with disabling conditions, there are some specific theological lessons to be learned from this parable. These lessons will not only influence how we perceive the Kingdom of God, but will also challenge and maybe reshape our current perceptions of those with disabling conditions, the very ones who are invited closest to the Host in the banquet of life.

A Common Gift For All: Grace Abounds

One of the most obvious lessons from this parable is that being part of God's Kingdom, Jesus tells us, is not based on good works and deeds, money and fame, but on God's gracious invitation. What is common among all the invited members is that they have been extended an invitation out of God's grace. The invitation is a gift extended by God to whom God wishes to invite. We are invited because we are a creation of God's love. The only way one can remain outside of the Kingdom is by turning down the invitation, and the support of the Christian community necessary in accepting God's gift of grace. As the New Testament theologian Joseph Fitzmyer writes, while we cannot save ourselves, we can very well damn ourselves.[169]

For the Church, this parable reveals that inclusion in God's Kingdom is not based on a model of individual good works and good deeds. Rather, it is based on God's gracious invitation, made known in the community of Christians. This is contrary to the implied message we send many people with disabling conditions and their families in Christian communities. Many congregations and parishes have excluded people with disabling conditions for the same reason that other social service agencies have segregated them. Many leaders in congregations determine whether a person with a disability may attend worship or Christian religious education activity by asking the question: "But can they get anything from the lesson?" or "But what can they *do* in worship or in our religious education program?" Such leaders lack the imagination to see that people with disabilities are God's children, as are people without disabilities, and already have been invited to take a seat or floor space in God's Banquet Feast on earth, the Church.

A Common Place Around the Table

What is interesting in the whole description is the idea that the table was big enough for all who were invited to sit at it and enjoy the meal. There is no sense that the table was overly crowded, with the need to move over to make an extra place for another person; in fact, there was so much space left over that the servant was sent out a second time to bring in more people.

This is an important point: If the banquet table is a metaphor for the Messianic banquet, the Kingdom of God, then people with disabilities have a place that already exists at the table. People with disabling conditions are not to be kept out of congregational life. They are to be warmly received.

This parable reminded me of our family's reunions, something I approached with conflicting feelings of joy and dread. For the most part, I enjoyed playing with the cousins my age. I dreaded the table arrangement used for these gatherings. There was the one table that was in the dining room that would only seat the adults. Meanwhile, the children were sent off to the smaller table in the kitchen to eat, make a mess, make noise, and cause just enough trouble to grab the attention of some of the adults at the dining table in the other room.

Many Christian communities use this same kind of table format, placing people with disabilities in a different room off of the place of worship. The reason? Because people with certain disabling conditions will not understand what is happening.

One pastor in Florida convinced other mainline denominational churches to bring all the people with mental retardation to the Masonic lodge on Sunday morning so that they could have worship just for those people with disabling conditions. When asked why these people should not attend the congregation that their family attended, this pastor responded that placing these people into a normal worship service, especially with a sermon, would be like placing them in a ninth-grade algebra class: "They [the people with mental retardation] wouldn't understand anything that was going on or being said." Many congregations have done the same thing.

A Common Reliance on God

In this parable, one of the common themes is the gathering's reliance on God, the One who created all of this in the first place; the One who extended the invitation and provided the table, the food, and the banquet hall.

This common reliance on God echoes throughout Scripture, both in the Old Testament and the New Testament. The Old Testament theologian Walter Brueggemann writes that Genesis 1 clearly indicates that all of creation is derived from and belongs to this sovereign, gracious God who will seek to have God's own way. God and creation are bound in a distinctive and delicate way, for nothing that lives has life and cannot sustain life without the Creator.[170]

For the Church, all members, no matter how seemingly gifted and talented, wealthy and famous, disabled and limited, have in common this reliance on God. All members around this Banquet Table, the Christian faith community, rely on God for the food that they eat, the houses they sleep in, the schools they attend, the therapy they receive, the clothes they wear. The list of ways we depend on God can roll on for quite some time. The basic point is that our very birth and being is a gift from God. And all of us rely upon God for all that we do.

A Common Life Shared with Others: Self-Embedded-in-Christian-Community

Everyone who comes to the banquet comes at their own pace and walking style, maybe needing a wheelchair, or the aid of a friend or help in eating or drinking. But no matter how they come or how they eat, all of this is symbolic of the larger message—that each person brings his or her unique being and presence. Instead of seeing each person as an individual, an atomistic entity that freely floats from relationship to relationship, there is a new way of perceiving each person, as a "self-embedded-in-Christian-community."

This is an important point gathered from all the descriptions and lessons of this Banquet Table parable. Each person, regardless of abilities or limitations, is important in the Kingdom of God. All have worth because God the Creator has made them.

Being part of God's creation and one of the invited guests at the Banquet Table means each person is a member of God's community—a group of people who share a history, share a place, share a common reliance on God for their very being. One's self is defined and described by being an active participant in this holy Christian gathering.

Because each person is part of this holy gathering, claiming this reliance on God around the common table of humanity, there should no longer be the threat of the scarcity paradigm. Instead of competing for health-service resources and help, there is equitable distribution of needed resources within our religious communities. Why? Because each person is part of this holy gathering that God has called into being. People in this setting go beyond what they think is possible in making life more comfortable, more caring, more compassionate, more accepting because of the shared vision of this banquet table, God's Holy Feast.

In conclusion, God extends an invitation to come to the banquet feast not because of what we do in life or what we individually get out of it. Those obviously talented, industrious, and creative individuals who we see as the "hard workers" of the Banquet Feast story were so caught up in their own agenda-filled lives that they failed to understand the most important opportunity that would come their way: They turned down the invitation to come to God's banquet not once, but twice. They didn't understand that God extended the invitation to these people because he enjoyed who they are, not because of what they do or what they own.

In the life of the Church, merely being in the presence of God may be truly threatening for some members at the Banquet Feast on earth. But this may be the prophetic message, the prophetic stance of many people with disabling conditions that renders the rest of us silent if not mute . . . this may be the correct position before the presence of God: merely being ourselves. Ultimately, God values human creation not because of what human beings can do but because they are created in the image of God, *imago Dei*.

Becoming God's Banquet Feast on Earth

What is it that God is doing among us, with us, and sometimes in spite of us? In the words of the Protestant reformers, God in Christ is still forming and reforming the Church to be the people of God that God in Christ wants us to be. In the spirit of this book, based on the image of God's Banquet Feast, God is helping our Christian communities to be and become more like God's Banquet Feast, encouraging and guiding us in the act of rearranging the seating pattern in our congregations and parishes so there is an invitation and plenty of room for people with disabling conditions to be welcomed and accepted around the table of our Lord. We get glimpses of what it may look like when we peek in during an evening meal at a l'Arche community, where people are gathered together at a common table, sharing a common meal, telling one another about what happened in their individual lives and how these things will have an impact on the rest of the community, since we are connected with one another through our bond with God.

Not only does God work in l'Arche communities, but also in our parishes and congregations, as we explore and discover the presence and place of people with disabling conditions in our Christian communities. As this parable of the Banquet Feast suggests, God is, in a sense, challenging our old assumptions about God's Kingdom and challenging our imaginations to think anew about God. This new perception warmly embraces and loves those who are now included, those whom many times, our congregations and parishes have excluded: people with disabling conditions. The parable makes it quite clear that everyone has a place at the banquet table. No one needs to make a new place; no other marginal group of people have to be squeezed out so that higher priority can be given to people with disabling conditions. No one who is already present in the life of a church needs to even move over. Instead, the task is discovering and recovering the place at the Messianic Banquet Table that God has already set aside for those people with disabling conditions.

Before moving on to explore the practical implications of this story, there are some closing thoughts that come from this discussion about God's banquet table:

First, there is the task of discovering and taking seriously the needs and concerns of the "unexpected guests" currently in the midst of our congregations and parishes. While many people with disabling conditions are present in churches, there appears to be almost willful ignorance of their concerns and those of their families. In some ways, people with disabilities feel that congregations would like to forget that they even exist.

For example, consider the story of Joanne, the mother of Jordie, who is 15 years old and is slightly developmentally delayed and emotionally disabled. Due to the developmental and emotional disabilities, Jordie had had many problems with the neighbors, never quite knowing where to draw the line between friendship and irritating nuisance.

Joanne remembers vividly going to her hometown church and asking her pastor for some support and guidance as she wanted to find out from the pastor where she should take her son for some counseling. She was hoping that she would get the name of a Christian psychiatrist in the area, and the pastor seemed to empathize with her plight as he shook her hand after church every Sunday morning after worship. Unfortunately, that's all that he did for Joanne—shake her hand and nod knowingly at her problems. He never returned her phone calls and pleas for help. When Joanne took Jordie to another church in the area, the youth pastor even met the boy and promised to come and visit him. But, again, there was no follow-up.

Many people with disabling conditions, sons and daughters in Christian communities, are hidden as parents feel self-conscious of their child's condition. In turn, they feel lonely and isolated rather than connected by common bonds. As for those who are disabled, many feel ignored, told through the inactions of a Church that they are not wanted, that there is little that the group can give them.

The "unexpected guests" are not only "out there" in the world, they are also "in here," in the midst of our very congregations and parishes, connected through certain members of the church. But their presence is hidden. And when not seen or heard from, they are ignored.

Second, as Christian communities, the task before us is to continually reimagine churches as God's Banquet Feast on earth.

One of the simplest yet most trying exercises in shaping our parishes and congregations so that they reflect more of this nature of inclusion is to care and provide for, work and live with, worship and grow with, be ministered to by people who have been labeled as being disabled. Yet we should be working with the *person* and not the disease or the limiting condition. This is a matter of envisioning anew the person who is, in part, disabled.

Another point, stated earlier in this chapter, is that this chapter and book are not promoting a socialization of faith, nor the idea that faith can happen through human efforts, or games we play in worship, or Christian religious education programs only. The premise of this book is that our collective work toward the inclusion of those who have been isolated from our faith communities is the first step toward being more like Jesus Christ. What is needed at first is a common image, a common vision, that has historical, theological, and biblical roots in order to believe that not only are those deemed by society as "disabled" to be included in Christian communities, but also—and more important—they are, in a sense, agents of change in this parable, helping those who see ourselves as "normal" and "able-bodied" understand that membership around the Banquet Feast of God is a result of God's gift of grace and out of human works.

Third, there is the issue of evangelism, of reaching out and extending an invitation to those with disabilities who have felt shut out and unwanted by many congregations and parishes.

The social philosopher Wendell Berry writes that love is always understood by others when it is expressed in concrete ways and not in abstract, metaphysical explanations:

> Love is never abstract. It does not adhere to the universe or the planet or the nation or the institution or the profession, but to the singular sparrows of the street, the lilies of the field, "the least of these my brothers and sisters."[171]

Like Berry's understanding of love, this parable is wonderful to talk about and discuss in abstract, theological language. But the reason that Jesus shared this parable in the first place was as a calling: Jesus is calling all Christian communities, throughout the ages, cultures, and reforms of churches, to understand that the Kingdom of God is made up of those whom we label as less fortunate and broken; those who are limited and disabled; those who are outcasts and misplaced in a world that places too much emphasis on fiscal success and healthy bodies.

If our congregations and parishes are to work on this model of inclusion, then Christian communities will have to change their current structures to finally discover that there is a place for people with disabling conditions.[172] There will need to be a "transformation of consciousness," new experiences in which our former boundaries and our limited perceptions are expanded and made more permeable because of God, the host of this Banquet.[173]

Christian communities will have to consciously acquire the skills to live out this vision, which may mean some changes in worship, in Christian religious education activities, in Christian fellowship time, in the very architectural structure of buildings, and in the organization of Christian communities. In order to do more for others, to maintain our common bond around this table, we will have to make changes in our collective lifestyles. Again, Wendell Berry suggests that the greatest obstacle in such a refashioned Christian community may be that we are dependent on what is wrong. As Berry claims: "This is the addict's excuse and will not do."[174]

There are some practical, concrete expressions and implications that need to be worked out in the life of communities of faith in order for them to be more like this Messianic Banquet. But these practical changes flow out of our sense of commonality and connection with others through and by God in Christ, where our efforts at change begin to seem logical and natural. As Jean Vanier writes about the church as a community of God and those in need:

> A community is only truly a body when the majority of its members is making the transition from "the community for myself" to "myself for the community," when each person's heart is opening to all the others, without any exception. This is the movement from egoism to love, from death to resurrection.[175]

In the coming chapters we will look at the practical issues congregations face as they learn to invite, welcome, and finally accept and celebrate the presence of the "unexpected guests," and as people discover that we are all members of Christ's community.

5

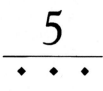

God's Banquet Feast
and the Church

At a small Christian liberal arts college, there was a campus-wide Disabilities Concerns Week dedicated to the issues and concerns of people with disabilities both in the wider society and on campus. For all practical purposes, the campus is not equipped with much in the way of adaptations for people with certain physical impairments who would be in need of such devices for independent living.

In the largest building on campus, where almost all the academic classes take place, there is no elevator connecting the three floors, nor are there any electronic doors. Why?

> An elevator in this hall would cost a minimum of $50,000. An elevator hasn't been brought up as a priority and the college hasn't "really felt the need for it at the moment. We are trying to make building more accessible," said the Physical Plant Director. And if the need arose, the problem of heavy doors could be alleviated by installing electric openers.[176]

"The college hasn't really felt the need for it at the moment." Replace the word "college" with "church" and one would have the same answer that many with disabling conditions have been given concerning accessibility into the physical structures of various churches. The above has also been the retort of many pastors, priests, lay leaders, Christian religious educators, pastoral counselors, and other concerned members of parishes and congregations when they are asked questions as to why the building, programs or worship are not more accessible to people with disabling conditions, especially those who need to use wheelchairs.

However, Christian congregations and parishes cannot rest that easy because of the biblical narrative and the situation of would-be believers. From a biblical perspective, one of the guiding visions for what the congregation is to be and become is God's Banquet Feast: God the Host has drawn up the guest list of this extraordinary meal that will capture our collective body, mind, and spirit. Because God has drawn up the guest list and told us, the living servants of Christ on earth, to go out and invite those with disabilities, we know what our mission is: "Go out into the streets and lanes of the town and bring in the poor, the crippled, the blind, and the lame" (Luke 4:21).

There is also a real need among people with disabilities to know that they are invited, welcomed, and accepted by a Christian community willing to learn what it will take to be a loving, caring, truth-seeking congregation. And one of the surest ways of making a guest or stranger know that the invitation is true and sincere is in a warm, embracing, enthusiastic welcome, where it is easy to enter or move around a building and where signs announce the joyous news that the guests have arrived. However, until our church buildings, worship, and Christian religious education programs are made inviting, accessible, and open to all who wish to enter and join in the life of a church, there is little chance that people with disabilities will be seen or heard from there. They will remain outside of the building, rejected from potluck affairs, excluded from worship, and left out of the religious education activities and pastoral ministry of our congregations. They will be more angry and bitter than ever.

Currently, there exists between Christ's community and communities of people with disabling conditions an angry division. This division has created a dispersion or diaspora, where the loosely bound community of people with disabilities has run away from or been rejected by many congregations and parishes. There are a scattered few congregations who have welcomed those with disabilities, and there are some communities of people who are disabled who feel welcomed. Yet overall, this scattering has left many with disabilities and their families with a sense of homelessness as they search for a church to welcome them.

Since this scattering has occurred, there is an eerie, audible silence.

that exists in communication between the community of God and the community of people with disabilities. Both communities feel hurt, sorrow, bitterness, despair, and woundedness. They often blame one another for these feelings. Both groups are timid about the plans for coming together around a common table, and about any other calls for a healing of relationships and lives. Both groups suffer, not because of their condition (whether the disability is visible or invisible), but because of the misperceptions and accompanying attitudes that are expressed through human action, no matter how wrong these actions are in light of God's gospel story. What is missing is not only trust but love and a spirit of forgiveness that people need in working out problems with one another.

True healing of the wounded relationship between the communities of those who are able bodied and those who are disabled can only come about when God's community lives and worships together in a common place. Only then will the Church truly resemble the nature of community as it is revealed in the Banquet Feast parable. As long as scattered members remain dispersed from a common place where they may talk with one another there can be no healing within communities of faith. Until that time, God's Banquet Feast has many empty seats as those with disabilities are often left outside, wandering in search of a community of meaning.

In this chapter, the focus is on preparing and stretching the collective imagination of the able-bodied participants to be a Christian congregation or parish desirous of inviting, welcoming, and accepting people with disabilities. To facilitate this spirit of welcome, the members of Christ's community will need some theological guidance and practical help in becoming more like the Banquet Feast. Having dealt with some of the theological issues for *why* churches should welcome those with disabilities, it is important to center on practical activities that are only the first steps in welcoming those who are left out. In the process, the suffering of people with disabling conditions, which comes about when people who are able bodied fail to consider and thereby reject the concerns of those who are disabled, will also be addressed.

The place for this new opening of hearts and minds is within the activities and occasions of a church's life. For example, congregational worship is an important time of practicing rituals in which there needs to be more inclusion of people with disabilities. It is in the rituals of

the life of the congregation where we take what the writer and natural-
ist Annie Dillard calls the stuff we have been doing since the year one
and do it again. [177] We, clumsily, try to worship God with our set pieces
of liturgy "as certain words which people have successfully addressed
to God without their getting killed."[178] God is stifling laughter at it
all. Perhaps God is also weeping at the reality that some people cannot
be included in and part of the body of Christ because of their physical,
physiological, mental, or sensory impairments. For God wants everyone
included at this Banquet Feast of love. It is incomplete without all
who wish to enter, sit or lie around, and sup on the "good food" of
God's love that is to be shared with all.

Another place that this opening will take place is in the Christian
religious education activities. It is in the pastoral ministry of the congregational life and in the Christian religious education programs that
true dialogue between children and adults, between those who are able
bodied and those who are disabled may take place. It is there that the
Spirit of God also resides. It is in the Christian religious education
program where our hearts, our minds, and our collective imagination
of our relationship with God is shaped and nurtured. As people of
God, we take our ordinary stories of life and discover new meaning as
we set our stories in the context of the sacred story as faithfully told
and lived out in the context of a worshipping community's praise of
God, particularly in Christian religious education program.

So far, many of the stories shared in this volume have been of pain
and rejection of people with disabling conditions and their families.
With the Banquet Feast in mind, it is important to read and hear
stories of hope and of the good things that are happening in many
congregations and parishes. What follows is a story about a family with
a child who is autistic, who were welcomed and accepted by a church.
In learning to worship with the child in their presence, the congregation became more like God's Kingdom on earth, learning to accept
the person for who she is, a child of God's, rather than for what she
could do in the Church.

Pointing the Way to the Banquet Feast

The storyteller is Patty, a mother who loves her daughter very much.
Her daughter, Annie, is a 12-year-old who is autistic and lives with
her family in a small house on the Idaho-Washington border.[179] Patty's

faith in Jesus' love for her daughter has enabled her to literally and figuratively move the bureaucratic mountains of state funds to meet the child's complex needs.

Yet Patty would not take all the credit when it comes to successfully obtaining the necessary programs for her daughter. She has done it with the help of a nearby small community church, which has been there for the family since they moved into this rural area a few years ago. There is Bill, "a man who likes to prophesy now and then," says Patty. He is part of the Transportation Team who take Annie to the nearby institution for what Patty's family calls a "Weekend of Normality." When Annie is home, another member of the church is the in-home care worker, helping Patty and Annie around the house. Norma, the careworker, got this job after her husband died last year of a heart attack. She needed some job to help supplement the small retirement benefits she was receiving. When she lost her husband, Norma felt very alone in her big house. Now, working with Patty and Annie, she once again feels some purpose in life.

This small parish is far warmer to Patty's family than the last church they attended in a different state. At the previous church, the pastor informed them that "this probably isn't the right church for you to come and worship in." His attitude proved that his words were right.

Patty emphasized that the church has been the most important and supportive at the times that she has to go on her journey in seeking funds, services, and adaptive equipment for her daughter. "Sometimes, it takes digging 15 or 16 holes in the ground to find the treasure that will help Annie. I need the support of the church to dig that one last hole, number 16, where the money is usually buried and hidden. The church has always been there with me while I've been digging."

In the context of congregational life, Patty stressed three stories that needed to be told and heard:

First, the story of Holy Saturday: On the Saturday after Good Friday and before Easter Sunday, Annie suddenly slipped out of the house and wandered off into the wilderness surrounding their house. When the family realized that Annie was lost, Patty called her prayer-chain for support. Soon, all 50 members were there at the house, helping the family look for Annie. What made this discovery mission particularly hard was that you cannot call some children with autism as easily as a normal child, especially Annie, who often seemed to ignore all human verbal commands. But toward the end of the evening, before it was dark, Annie was found, with the help and support of the prayer-chain "search team."

Second, in the life of the small, traditional community church the family attends, Annie is quite "charismatic." She has been known to go running in front of the church, dancing around the pulpit. The pastor takes it in stride, smiling, acknowledging that Annie is there, and continuing to preach without missing a beat.

Third, no one in the church can speak in tongues. Yet the pastor's daughter was sure that must have been what was happening when Annie, during the time of silent prayer, let out a string of garbled vowels and consonants that made no logical, grammatical sense.

Fourth, more than once Annie has simply deserted her family in the church, to be found wandering around in the hallways. Many times she ends up in the nursery. Once she was found naked there. Another family was heard to say, as they passed by the classroom and shielded their eyes: "Yep, Annie's here for church," as they just walked on to the sanctuary.

In Patty's mind, the church has learned to accept Annie just as she is. They let her go to the front of the line at the church potlucks and eat whatever and wherever she wants. She went to Vacation Bible School with her older sister one summer, and, according to Patty, "She did O.K. with just playing with the arts-and-crafts stuff, ignoring the rest of the lesson and the children in the class."

What has happened in the life of this congregation is that they have, consciously or unconsciously, chosen to live with Annie and her different actions and reactions. And Annie, by willingly going to church, has chosen to attend. It is important to remember that if Annie, even though she is autistic, did not want to go to church, she could have put up enough of a chaotic, frenzied fuss that would have deterred even the most determined of families.

The reason that Patty was so determined to find a church that accepted the whole family is that she knew, deep inside her, that it was right that the whole family worship God in Christ together. She thought that there is something fundamentally wrong in the life of a congregation or parish when a person cannot attend and be part of worship because of what he or she does, or looks like, or acts.

Rules and norms concerning social etiquette in congregations and parishes have been challenged throughout biblical times and the Church's history: In Hebrew Scriptures, we are told of King David dancing naked before the Ark of the Covenant. Psalm 150 commands the children of God to worship God not in silence but with trumpet sounds, lutes, harps, tambourines, dance, strings, pipes, clanging, and clashing cymbals: "Let *everything* that *breathes* praise the Lord" (Psalm 150:6). That appears to be one of the only rules for worship of God— the ability to breathe, which would clearly include even those with disabling conditions. Worship may be quite a raucous yet celebrative occasion, where the participants physically, emotionally, cognitively, and spiritually relinquish themselves to God.

Another important part of this story is both the determination of parents like Patty in bringing their children with disabilities to worship God, and the transformation of sorts that occurred with the inclusion of the child with the disabling condition in the church itself. Patty has found that she has to search and search to find the hole with the treasure of support and financial funds to keep Annie at home. And she is determined to make it possible for her child to stay at home with her family as long as it is financially, physically, emotionally, and spiritually possible.

The transformation of congregational life occurred in the church as it learned to accept "the stranger," one who was utterly different, as one of their own in Christ Jesus. Patty's congregation is now accustomed to Annie's walking around in the front of the chancel area during the preaching of the sermon, to Annie's voluntary prayers, and to Annie's presence in the nursery school.

More congregations and parishes are learning to live and worship with people who are disabled, particularly with those who are mentally retarded or mentally ill. For example, what I heard was happening in Patty and Annie's church was happening in congregations and parishes that welcomed members of l'Arche communities. In the l'Arche community in London, many attend a very traditional Anglican church in the neighborhood. I remember the many times that Rose, who is mentally retarded, would stand up and walk out of worship when she needed to use the bathroom, with the priest never missing a beat in the sermon.

In the same congregation, all was formal, rather stuffy, and precise in the liturgy, until the passing of the peace. With that, Sue, a woman with mental retardation, would stand straight up and, at the top of her voice, cheerily greet others in the name of Christ. "How *are* you, darling?" she would say as she'd embrace a complete stranger in the

Anglican parish. The air of worship itself became more alive and re-laxed with Sue's embraces and greetings as the clergy and parishioners would follow her example, filling the sanctuary with the peace of Christ.

What these stories point to is one of the reasons that we come to worship as a congregation. In one sense, the reason people gather together is to worship God and learn of God's ways for Christ's people. In the next section, there will be a discussion of ways to enable churches to become places where even those with disabilities may wor-ship God. With such learning goals and moments, the church is touch-ing on what the Christian religious educator Thomas Groome calls the meta-purpose of Christian religious education: to lead people into the kingdom of God as proclaimed and lived out by Jesus Christ.[180] Chris-tian religious education is about the task of instructing the congrega-tion's collective imagination to be more like God's kingdom, the Banquet Feast, here on earth. The invitation to come to the banquet has been sent out and proclaimed by the servant, Jesus Christ, compel-ling everyone to come to God's Banquet, for all is ready.

God's Banquet and Christian Religious Education for the Church

Christian communities can no longer afford to live life without peo-ple with disabilities, for they are the invited guests to God's Banquet Feast. The Church's goal involves being and becoming a place for all who wish to worship rather than just for those with or without certain abilities and limitations.

The hope of this vision of God's Banquet Table is that two groups are necessary in order to finally be one in God. If a congregation is composed of just people who are seemingly able bodied, things are incomplete. If a congregation is comprised of those who have one kind of disabling condition, the gathering is still incomplete. For the Ban-quet Table to be complete, there needs to be the Host and the guests.

In order to become more like God's Banquet Feast, congregations and parishes will have to do the following:

Extend an Invitation to the Banquet

The first thing that the Host does in preparing for this grand Banquet is to invite guests. In Luke 14:13–24, Jesus tells those who are listening to the parables about the invitations and who should and should not be invited.

This is a crucial point to begin with in terms of welcoming people into a community, and one that is quickly sidestepped. For example, there are congregations and parishes that do not have people with disabling conditions coming to them, even some that have wheelchair ramps, braille Bibles, large-print bulletins, and adaptive equipment for those with hearing impairments. Why? Because they forgot the first step of *inviting* people with disabilities.

To invite the stranger into the midst of a Christian community is a risk. To invite someone who isn't like you and me may disturb a church's routine, shaking up the comfort or the status quo of a gathering. Jean Vanier, the founder of l'Arche, has observed that opening the doors of a community is also opening the doors of our hearts, where human beings are most vulnerable. Inviting the stranger, the one who is disabled, into our lives is not only a necessary outward gesture in integrating our communities, but an inner attitude. It means welcoming them and making them feel at home, in their place within the community of faith.[181]

Welcome the Invited Guests to the Banquet

Jesus is clear in the parables surrounding the banquet table that when the invitations have been extended and the guests are coming, those who are the strangers in the crowd, particularly those with disabilities, should be made to feel welcomed with the most distinguished places at the table (Luke 14:14).

To welcome the stranger, in this case the one who is disabled, reveals that what is essential in the Kingdom of God is love, because the stranger may be viewed as one who is God sent, like Christ who came as a stranger into the world, born in a lowly manger.[182] The Christian community is to welcome the stranger, which is love; love is most clearly present in the Christian obligation to be hospitable to the stranger.[183]

In some Christian households, the rule of hospitality is to accept the stranger as a guest unconditionally, with no questions asked concerning the origin or station in life of the stranger. In other primitive religions, the stranger was to be welcomed as an honored guest because he or she may be a god in disguise. Other times, the saints and hermits of the early Church even treated strange, wild animals with reverence because God, the One who created all living things, is also part of the land humankind occupies.[184] By the very act of being hospitable to the stranger or guest, one is sharing what one has already been given, and, in a sense, rendering to God our thanksgiving for what has been generously offered.[185]

To Accept and Care for the Guests at the Banquet

In the parable of the banquets, Jesus makes the point that those people who had been the outcasts of Jewish society, those with obvious disabling conditions, should feel not only welcomed but accepted and should be cared for by the Host. It is around the table of the Great Banquet that people are fed, physically, spiritually, and emotionally; they are finally satisfied, feeling healed through the wondrous gift of grace and love given by the Host. Around this love feast, people with disabilities and those who are able bodied alike feel accepted and cared for as God's children.

Care is essential for the daily function of life in a community. We need to care for others as well as to be cared for by others in certain times of our lives. It is not only or always people with disabilities who are going to be recipients of care. Being on the receiving end of care makes one dependent on the good works of another person. Those who are seemingly able bodied are struck by the barriers and narrow-mindedness of their own lives when they are cared for by people who are disabled. It is in the act of caring, of accepting one another as human beings with a variety of abilities and limitations, supporting one another, challenging each other to grow, being and acting responsible for the well-being of the community, that the gathering truly becomes more like God's Banquet Feast.

Activities Around God's Banquet Feast

In light of the fact that it is easier to read and write about such broad goals in the church than to accomplish them, this next section centers on activities that communities may use.

A few words of caution in using these activities:

First, the goal of these activities is not to give a total experience of what it is like to be disabled in a largely non-disabled world. The only way one can truly experience this is by being disabled. None of us can truly understand what it is to have Down's syndrome unless we have the condition, or what it is like to be dead weight in a wheelchair unless we are in it for the rest of our lives. Instead, the hope is that the members of a congregation will be aware of the needs and concerns of people with disabling conditions, and that these needs and concerns may be more easily addressed and perhaps remedied within the confines of a community's life. The first step is admitting that there is a need; the next step is the creative problem solving that needs to take place with the persons with disabilities as part of the planning team.

Second, this chapter is written with an eye for growth and process. There are going to be awkward moments as the community of God works toward learning to live and worship with those who are disabled. Like anything that is being learned, there are going to be some rough moments when a church tries to communicate and explore the needs of those with disabilities in the context of the Christian community. It is prudent to begin with simple, less threatening, almost silly ideas, and step off from there toward activities that will make individual members and the congregation as a whole reflect on the ways we have excluded those with disabilities in our collective past.

Third, it is assumed that many of the largely non-disabled members of a congregation will focus on how they too are individually and communally disabled in some sense. Whether one is wearing glasses or a hearing aid, or unable to complete some subjects in school, or has a physiological condition that is a problem, many maladies begin to surface. Personal identification with those who are disabled is a common reaction among those who seem able-bodied. For some, this eases the uncomfortable awkwardness that arises when meeting and confronting a person who is disabled. For others, this self-revelation is in some sense cathartic, bringing a sense of relief to finally be talking with someone who has a disabling condition that may have fascinated the person who is able bodied. And the other reaction is one of laughter and jokes. Humor, in this case, seems to release much of the anxiety and insecurity that emerge as people learn to live with those who are different from you and me. These appear to be fairly typical reactions to people with disabilities.

Fourth, many of these activities are meant for the Christian religious education programs of congregations and parishes. They may be adapted to work with a group of preschoolers, children in the elementary and secondary ages, and youth groups and adult Christian religious education courses. They are all activities that are typically known as "hands-on" in the education vernacular, leading to a discussion follow-ing the activity. There is also one section of activities and suggestions for inclusive worship.

Fifth, if the sense of "being disabled like you and me" is not the goal of these activities, then what is the purpose of these exercises? To relax among people who happen to be disabled. When talking with the cartoonist and writer John Callahan, himself a quadriplegic, about what he would like to say to a college audience regarding disabilities, his last word was: Relax.[186] Just know that people with disabilities are no different than you or me; in truth, we are all more alike than different. Perhaps one way to think about a disabling condition, be it mental retardation, physical disability, or mental illness, is as *another* way of seeing the world, or what the writer Graham Greene, using Shakespeare, said was another form of inspiration: "Much madness is divinest sense . . . that sort of thing."[187]

People with disabilities are people, created in the image of God. As members of the human race, they are also as easily manipulative of others and vicious toward one another as anyone else. They know how to put on the "act" of being disabled to make those who are able bodied feel guilty. There is, among the community of people with disabilities, a degree of "learned helplessness," where the person appears to be unable to learn some rather simple chores. The way to overcome some of the manipulations of some people with disabilities is to know the person as a human being, just like any other member of a congregation or parish, a part of God's creation. People with disabilities have their moments of wonder and brilliance, and their times of limitations and deficiencies. To relate to one another as human beings, to avoid and get away from the labels that only hide us, is the hope of this work.[188] In other words, "they" are "us."

Finally, the activities are not put in any order, as from difficult to easy. They are to be adapted for the gathering that has decided to become more aware of those unexpected guests at God's Banquet Table. The hope is that people will laugh, reflect on the activity, and think about it from both the perspective of the non-disabled participant and the member who is disabled. Even reading stories of the sacred story, the Bible, takes on new meaning when read from the vantage point of one who is disabled. Give the activities some time to sink in; don't rush the teaching moment. Provide people an opportunity to express the hurt, the pain, the silliness, the wonder, and the burden of being disabled in a society that envisions itself, by and large, as nondisabled, no matter how much of a myth this position. Ask people to give thought and reflection to God's lovingly empathetic response to the pain of being disabled. Congregations should be prepared to open up the doors of our sanctuaries and the doors of our minds and hearts to the presence of unexpected guests at God's Banquet Feast.

Name Game!

An important introduction to all of the activities is this cathartic experience of writing down on either an overhead or a piece of butcher paper, in large print, all of the names or labels that have been used in schools, playgrounds, ballparks, churches, synagogues, Boy and Girl Scouts, and so on regarding people with disabilities. It is always amazing to find out what hurt-filled names we call one another. This list would most likely include or begin with some old gems like retard or tard, moron, imbecile, handicapped, differently abled, physically challenged, fool, feeble-minded, "microcephalic idiot," gimpy, spaz, schiz, neurotic, paranoid, dwarf, and munchkin-head.

The reason that this activity may be so cathartic is that it brings an idea of how prevalent these terms are in the general society, including our religious gatherings. It is usually not until someone holds up the term and names the expression that people are aware of the biases they have been living with and promoting.

To put this "name calling" into perspective, read Psalm 139:13–18. In this passage, we read that God lovingly formed us, carefully knitting us together in our mother's womb. God knows us for who we are, not by the names that others have attached to us.

God's Banquet Table

The goal of this activity is to prepare and eat a dinner with people who are non-disabled and people with a disabling condition. You may choose to read Jesus' parable of the Banquet Table in Luke 14:15–24 in preparation for the adventure that is about to begin.

First, select or choose pairs around one table that is big enough for a whole group. In some settings, you may have to pair people off. In these dyadic relationships, one person is going to role-play that he or she has a disability, while the other person role-plays the non-disabled person. For the person who is disabled, provide some bandages and slings so that, for example, a person's eyes are covered, symbolic of one who is visually impaired. Others may have cotton in or headphones on their ears, which will simulate the experience of hearing impairment. Tying participants' hands behind their backs will approximate the experience of the person without arm mobility. Or have one person wear a shirt that is too long and tie off the sleeves to remind them of a person who has no use of hands.

The role of the person who is non-disabled is to help the person with the disabling condition. The key to the exercise is that the person who is non-disabled will need to wait for the person who is disabled to give the cues of how he or she wants to or needs to be aided in the activity of eating a meal. The person who is hearing impaired will have to figure out hand signs for "talking" about what the person with the hearing impairment wants to eat for dinner. The person who is blind will need help in finding out where all the utensils are. And the person who is physically impaired will need help in eating the food, drinking from a cup, and using a napkin. Try this activity, from coming to sit at the table, to saying a prayer before the meal, to finding out what is served, to serving the food, to eating and cleaning up afterward. There really is a trick to getting everyone fed and happy.

This experience will give a taste of the frustration many people with certain disabling conditions feel when trying to negotiate a meal in an able-bodied world. There is a trick to opening a straw wrapper and getting a drink with it if you don't have the use of your hands—asking another person to help with the straw. It is a task to get someone to pass the salt if you cannot speak or hear. There is work involved in learning exactly where the edge of the plate is when you don't have any perceptual idea of what you are eating from—many times people end up eating off of the table. Be sure to have some time to discuss the feelings and perceptions both from the perspective of the one who is "disabled" and the one who is "able-bodied."

Disabled Like Me!

This is a variation on God's Banquet Table. It's a simulation exercise that has worked with many Christian religious education classes and youth groups. The goal is to get a glimpse of what it is like to walk and talk around a congregation or parish with a disabling condition. Again, select pairs for this activity, maybe counting off so all the "ones" and "twos" know who they are paired with. One person may have a blindfold over his or her eyes, and will need to be guided through the building. Another person may have headphones on and the partner will learn to communicate with the hearing impaired person through a series of their own crafted hand and facial signs. Borrow some wheelchairs and crutches for walking around a building, with the person who is able bodied helping with doors and stairs. For the person on crutches, tie either the right or left leg up so that they have no use of the one leg. Get a long-sleeved shirt for a person who has no use of hands. For people with a learning disability, have them write their name. To portray a person with a learning disability these people write their name while sitting with their back to the wall on a piece of newsprint taped to the wall behind them. It is very disorienting for the "disabled" person to write by this method.

Be sure that people have more than a few minutes to try this activity out. If it could last for a day, this would be ideal, including the arduous and embarrassing issues of going to the bathroom, washing up after a meal, walking around a church or a campus in an uncomfortable, compromising position. Feel free to switch roles some time in the activity. Have plenty of time to talk about the perspective of being "disabled" and "able-bodied." Also, since this may be done in public, talk about the reaction of others around the pair, whether people stared or laughed at the situation.

"If I Were Disabled . . ."

This activity may be performed in a church or a camp setting. Take a 5-by-8-inch piece of paper and at the top of it write in big, bold, print: "IF I WERE DISABLED . . ." Then fill in the rest of the paper with a disabling condition and a real-life challenging situation. Here are a few examples:

"IF I WERE DISABLED . . ." and had a hearing impairment, could I hear what was being discussed in this Sunday school class?

"IF I WERE DISABLED . . ." and had a visual impairment, could I read the church bulletin?

"IF I WERE DISABLED . . ." and was in a wheelchair, could I get up this flight of stairs or into this fellowship hall?

"IF I WERE DISABLED . . ." and was quadriplegic, could I open the manual door to the church office?

"IF I WERE DISABLED . . ." and had cerebral palsy, could I participate in the activities of this youth group?

"IF I WERE DISABLED . . ." and had AIDS, would you let me into this congregation or parish?

"IF I WERE DISABLED . . ." and was schizophrenic, would you let me worship with you?

Put these signs up in front of the Sunday School classroom, in front of the worshipping area, by the room where the youth group meets, or by the church office. It would be good to have some time with those who participated in the activity as a group, to discuss what some of the reactions. When this was tried on a college campus, some people were so bothered by the signs that the students took them down because they knew there was little they could do about the physical structure of the school.

Of the World and Being in the World

This is a collage project, where the group gathered together would have two large pieces of newsprint or butcher paper, scissors, glue, and a pile of magazines and newspapers. On one piece of newsprint, write the words, "DISABLED" at the top, and on the other piece of newsprint write the words, "ABLE-BODIED" at the top. For the "Disabled" poster, find all the pictures and slogans found in our print media that typify how people in the world view those with disabling conditions. Search for pictures of people in wheelchairs, those with glasses on, those using canes, or those who have hearing aids. On the "Able-Bodied" poster, find pictures of those who are able bodied and do not have a disabling condition that we can visibly see.

What is interesting about this project is that, first, there are fewer pictures of people in pain or with a disability than those who are able bodied. In society, especially in advertisements, there are more pictures of people who are able bodied. Second, the pictures of those who are disabled are usually frowning or looking uncomfortable, while those who are able bodied are usually in great shape and smiling. Discuss with the group how these very images reflect society's concept of those with disabling conditions, and how these images shape and nurture our bias toward them. Our perspective toward those with disabilities is shaped by the pictures that society places around us.

The Labeling and Categorizing Game

This activity may be done in Christian religious education programs with children to adults, and with youth groups. In a gathering of six or more people, place a piece of masking tape on the forehead of each person in the group with a different disabling condition written on each piece of tape. Have the group choose an activity for a Friday night.

Some of the examples for the labels or signs may be: "I'm Deaf," "I'm Blind," "I'm Autistic," "I'm Mentally Retarded," "I Have Cerebral Palsy," "I Have AIDS," "I Have A Heart Condition." This may need to be accompanied by a description of how the disability manifests itself in the human body, for example, cerebral palsy.

Gather this group of five to ten people with these signs on their forehead without anyone seeing the individual condition labeled on their own tape as they sit facing one another. Now have the group treat one another in the manner that they would actually treat or relate with a person with that disabling condition. The goal of each individual is to guess what condition they have been labeled with by observing how they are treated by the rest of the members of the group. For example, the person who is hearing impaired may figure out that he is deaf by people trying to speak slowly and loudly to him. A person with cerebral palsy may figure out that she has a physical condition by people helping her stand and sit down. We become, in a certain sense, the condition that we are labeled in life. There is a sense of self-fulfilling prophecy involved in this game.

After 20 to 30 minutes of this game, have each person try to guess what his or her label says by telling the members of the group how they were treated by others. Discuss how easily we fall into relating to one another as the labels we use.[189]

This Place Is Off-Limits

To give people a sense of the physical and attitudinal barriers in a community, try this activity. Close off all the doors to a church during worship, except for one. Don't lock the doors in case there is a fire or an emergency. Have one door, usually the one that is hardest to get to or the most awkward to open. Or perhaps tape off the nearest stairway entrance to a church office, library, or youth group room.

Another idea is to make a maze of stairs and inner tubes from old tires that people have to walk through in getting to their destination in the building.

The point of the example is easy: For some people in a wheelchair or with cerebral palsy life appears to be one great obstacle course. It can be frustrating to negotiate the easiest entrances to a building, which are sometimes in the back.

Getting Behind Our Masks

Part of being human, an awareness of our very human condition is that we are all broken and limited in what we can do and who we are in the presence of God's love. We are disabled by sin. Being vulnerable with one another, allowing another person to see what we are like behind the mask that we commonly show one another in our ordinary lives, is challenging. In this activity, the goal is to identify those things that we do well, revealing our gifts and talents to one another on one side of our mask. On the other side of our mask, the inner self, we reveal what our limitations and foibles are, our shortcomings and inadequacies, those things that others would see as a disability, a "handicap" in life.

For this project, cut out of construction paper face masks to cover the whole face, cutting out the place where our eyes, nose, and mouth should be. Provide enough yarn to tie the mask around each person's head, or have sturdy tagboard and place a stick behind the mask so that one can hold the mask up with the stick. Bring plenty of feathers, scraps of paper, clay, magazines, newspapers, glue, scissors, tape, staples, paint and brushes, colored markers, and string.

On the outside of the mask, have each person choose symbols and pictures that communicate to others what their abilities, talents, and gifts are, as perceived by themselves. They may include scenes of water skiing; a picture of a violin for a musician; a picture of a gourmet meal for a cooking enthusiast; or a book for an avid reader. For the inside of the mask, choose pictures that demonstrate or symbolize one's sinful condition or what the person cannot do—choose images and pictures of one's limitations and deficiencies. Some may choose an athletic activity that they cannot accomplish; a mathematical equation they cannot solve; a book they cannot see or read. They may choose a picture of an abused, hungry child symbolizing the child within who feels abused.

After creating these masks, gather together in a small group and share them with one another. Allow each person to share however much he or she wants to. This is a powerful activity as people may expressed some inner thoughts and perceptions that they have never shared before. In trying this exercise, it is helpful to have the group read the prophecy of Jeremiah in the Old Testament. Read Jeremiah 1:4-10, where God is telling the reluctant Jeremiah that God has chosen him to speak, and that God will, metaphorically, put the words into his mouth. In the same sense, it is God who chooses to use each person and who gives God's children the energy and words that will change lives. This is not predicated on our estimation of our abilities but on God's judgment of the human heart. God knows what is in front of and behind the masks we wear . . . and loves us anyway.

Alike and Different!

This is a simple song that has been used in music therapy activities for many years. Have a small group gathered together in a circle facing one another. Have them chant the following lyrics, which are quite simple:

> Alike and different!
> Alike and different!
> We are alike and dif-fe-rent!

Have people clap hands to the rhythm of the activity, or alternate between clapping their own hands and those of the people next to them.

At the end of the chant, have a person in the group turn to the person on her or his right and give an example of how they are alike and an example of how they are different. It may be that they are alike in that they both wear glasses, and that they are different in that one is a boy and the other is a girl.

The goal of this activity is to explore with a group of people how we are all alike in some respects, and how we are different from one another. There is value in both the ways we are alike and the ways we are different!

The Un-Slide Show

The purpose of this slide show is to help a group of people become aware of the physical and attitudinal barriers that exist in this world with people who are disabled. No words or songs should be part of this slide show: focus on the pictures and try to find out the message behind the scenes. Don't tell anyone what the theme of the slide show is going to be. Just sit back, relax, and critically reflect on the slides' messages.

Include in this slide show pictures of cars without a "handicap parking" permit parked in a "Handicapped" parking space outside of a store or a mall. Take pictures of people using canes and walkers, wheelchairs and crutches. In between these pictures have random pictures of natural scenes. Take a picture of a preschool or elementary school with children who are disabled in the play area. Go to a medical office and take pictures of those who are coming in and out of the building. Take pictures of those using the wheelchair ramps outside of buildings, perhaps with a skateboarder coming down the ramp. Take pictures of large stairways outside of churches and libraries; take photos of doors that are not electric. Take pictures around the library where there could be braille books or large-print books.

Then have the whole group discuss the themes and messages of the slide show. Include a reading from Matthew 25, focusing on what we do for the least of our brothers and sisters. What were some of the common images that the group saw flashed on the screen? Ask the group to find the logical thread that connects the whole slide show. Hopefully, the viewers will focus on the issues confronting many with disabilities. Discuss ways that some of the barriers could be removed for those with disabling conditions with the help of those who are able bodied.

What a Body!

How do we look to others? What do we look like to ourselves? And what would it be like if we didn't have a certain part of our body? How would the larger body—for Christians, the image of the body of Christ—respond to one another's needs? The group may begin this activity with a reading of the Apostle Paul's letter to the Corinthians in 1 Cor. 12:12-31 which focuses on the many gifts of the body of Christ. Each person is important in the body of Christ as each one plays a vital role in the overall healthy functioning, regardless of how obtuse or unnecessary each part appears to those outside of the Church.

In this project for children and adults in a Christian religious education setting, each person is going to draw. In this exercise, get enough butcher paper, crayons, and scissors for the group. Have each person lay down on a piece of paper while someone else traces around their body. Cut off the excess paper so that you have just the outline of the body. Fill in the body parts with crayon and paper, putting clothes and a face on this empty slate.

Seeing the outline of one's body is a powerful image. Though a rough shadow of one's self, it is, nonetheless, a copy of how one looks. There will be some nervous giggling along with some silence by others. Give the group time to process what they just created with this work of art.

Once everyone is finished with their body, have each person sit by the side or on top of their paper body. Suggest to one person that she or he make black frame glasses or an eye patch for the eyes. Discuss what it would be like not to have the gift of sight, and then ask the questions, "How can others in the circle help the one without sight?" Write down the suggestions for care on a piece of paper. For another person, cut off the two legs, or fold them up under the paper outline, and talk about what they could and couldn't do without legs. Again, have the group talk about ways of supporting this individual without legs. Or have everyone fold a leg up, and talk about mobility when everyone needs a crutch.

Finish this time with a reading from 1 Corinthians 12. Discuss with the group how the larger body, the group, can work together and be with one another, supporting one another even when one thinks or perceives they are weak and have nothing to give to the larger body.

There are two purposes of this activity: first, that even if we didn't have a body that was fully functional, it would not be the "end of the world." Second, as long as we are part of a loving community of God, then we can all support and be with one another. That gives each person strength and hope to last a lifetime.

The Disability Music Band

Along with the Apostle Paul's image of Christ's body as a paradigm for the church found in 1 Corinthians 12, this activity reinforces how essential each person is in the functioning of the community of faith, with each adding a gift to create a sound that is full and unique, and that would be less than satisfying without one of the parts.

Borrow a box of rhythm instructions from a preschool or elementary school. You may use Orff-Kodaly xylophones and drums as well afor this activity. Give each person a different instrument. Around the neck of each person, have a sign identifying them with a disabling condition. There should be signs for a person with a hearing impairment, a visual impairment, mental retardation, mental illness, and a physical disability. Have the group then play music to the song, "Kum-Ba-Yah," or another easy song, with each person contributing her or his unique sound.

Now remove an instrument, like the tambourine that might represent a person who is blind, and play the song. There's an essential flourish missing without the tambourine. Now take out a drum, played perhaps by a person with a physical disability. There's a missing bass beat without a drum. In other words, without all the instruments in the band playing the song, there's always going to be "something missing." Each person, no matter how innocuous or simple he or she seems, is important within God's creation of this human band. God desires to have a complete band, with all the instruments. Play the tune with everyone again participating and banging their musical character. Enjoy the parade!

Worshipping God

So far, most of the activities have been oriented toward the Christian religious education programs in traditional Sunday school sessions. Many of the above activities are more suited to younger people than the older, adult members of a church. However, as was mentioned earlier in this book and chapter, the primary place where Christian religious education takes place is in the context of worship among the older and younger congregants. There is much written and available about activities and programmatic changes that can be made in congregations and parishes when they are in worship. In the book, *Creating the Caring Congregation,* the Rev. Harold Wilke proposes that one Sunday a year be established as "Access Sunday," when the needs and concerns of people with disabling conditions be front and center in the minds of the worshippers.[190] Some parishes and congregations have incorporated some very simple ideas in worship so that more people with disabling conditions may feel comfortable in worshipping God among those who are able bodied. Some of these activities are as follows:

• **"Let Us Please Sit"**: At the bottom of some church bulletins, an asterisk explains "Please stand if you so wish or are able," so that those who are in wheelchairs or holding sleeping babies will not feel out of place among others who are standing.

This issue of standing, sitting, and kneeling is important for those with bad backs or for those who have problems with their knees. For some people, it is easier to just sit, and the standing and kneeling that goes on in some churches during worship is taxing. It is possible that some of the hymns of the church could be sung while sitting down, as could some of the creeds and prayers that are recited by the gathering in unison. Try sitting for an entire worship service for an idea of what it would be like to be in a wheelchair or to be unable to walk.

• **Silence in the Congregation:** One activity that has been tried in some congregations and parishes is whispering parts of the liturgy so that people really have to strain to hear what is being said. By whispering through parts of the worship service, people who have good hearing have to work hard on hearing what is being said by the priest, pastor, - or lay leader. This provides a taste of what it is like to have a hearing impairment and attend worship in an able-bodied congregation.

• **Movement with Music:** One change in worship that has an impact on a worshipping community is when an interpreter for those who are deaf or hearing impaired is invited to come and sign the worship service. The inclusion of one who knows American Sign Language provides a wonderful addition to worship, giving the words of the hymns, prayers, and sermons a truly concrete expression. More importantly, it is providing those who have hearing impairments or are deaf an opportunity to receive the message for the day.

It is also moving to have the parish or congregation sign to one another if there is an interpreter present. Using American Sign Language or cued speech in worship makes it more possible for all to receive and reflect on God's sacred story in their lives, regardless of their abilities or limitations.

• **In Search of Light:** Another way of enabling a congregation to be aware of the needs of people with disabilities, especially those with visual impairments and blindness, is to dim the lights within the worship area so low that people have to struggle to read the words printed in the hymn book or the Bible.

Perhaps one way of awakening people to the needs of those who have visual problems, like cataracts and tunnel vision, is to print the bulletin and the congregation's or parish's newsletter in large print. Many elderly members with visual impairments will thank the committee who designed the larger print. Many copiers have a button to enlarge the print of the bulletins and newsletters.

Another activity is to have part, if not all, of the bulletin for worship translated and coded in braille, the raised-dots method used in helping people with visual impairments read. Again, this is a new language for many people to learn and try to accommodate in their ordinary life experience.

• **Incense and the Bells:** An idea borrowed from my Roman Catholic and Episcopalian brothers and sisters will, for many Protestant congregations and parishes, be a new experience. For many children who are mentally retarded or those who are autistic, and maybe for those who are multiply disabled, one of the senses that is functioning is the sense of smell. When the Gospel story is read in worship, begin to use the incense, putting the pot that holds the incense somewhere around the one reading the Bible. Have the children and adults with or without disabilities gather around the reader of the Scripture. Have the children with disabilities touch the Bible, holding it as someone reads the words. Use plenty of bells during Holy Communion or the Lord's Supper, announcing what is happening. Many of those who are lower functioning in terms of their cognitive understanding of the world will often respond to the smells and bells of worship.

• **The Songs of Worship:** The songs we sing in churches play a fundamental role in shaping the theological perspective of the participants singing and listening to the words of the hymns. When my daughter was three years old, she was already mouthing the words to "Jesus loves me" because "the Bible tells me so."

But there are some hymns that do not include everyone with a disabling condition. There is the hymn, "Rise Up, O Men of God." Imagine singing songs about people doing things that you will never do from a wheelchair. Or there is a hymn that connects deafness with ignorance: "Ye deaf and dumb." We need to pay attention to how hymns shape the very perspective members of a Christian community at prayer have of God and the world as communicated and interpreted by some of the hymn writers.

A final word about worship: As we include activities during our liturgies that are more tactile and kinesthetic, stimulating more of the senses, more people with certain limitations that we would call disabling are able to participate in worshipping God. The neuropsychiatrist and writer Oliver Sacks wrote that people with mental retardation live in a world of concreteness: "Their world is vivid, intense, detailed, yet simple, precisely because it is concrete: neither complicated, diluted, nor unified, by abstraction."[191] Not only those who are disabled will be able to express and receive more of the message of worship, be it the sacred stories of the Old Testament and the New Testament, but so are the children and a larger group of those who are elderly.

These activities are most essential when a church begins reaching out to people with disabilities—when the ramp for the wheelchair is being built and the sign language interpreter is found. They are intended to awaken congregants and parishioners to the needs and concerns of others within their midst. However, even the best of intentions may lose appeal, and something more substantial is required for the long haul.

Both the pastoral leadership of the Church, including the Christian religious educator, and the people with disabilities with their friends and family, will need to encourage more theological reflection on this issue in the various parts of life in a church. Congregational and parish leadership need to use sermons, seminars, book studies, newsletters, mailings, church library book selections, lectureships, and workshops to broaden people's awareness about the concerns of people with disabling conditions. The entire spectrum of disabling conditions and the vulnerability many feel—even the vulnerability and brokenness of God as revealed in Jesus on the cross—must be critically examined by all the members of Christ's community.

Some practical movements that may be made in churches whether they are beginning to welcome people with disabilities into congregations and parishes or they are already including people with disabilities, are:

First, offer classes now and then in Sunday school or adult religious education courses on disabling conditions. Such a course would explore the history as well as current research on various disabling conditions so that parishioners will be educated about what some people are living with in their daily life.

Second, make brochures, pamphlets, videos, audiotapes and books about disabling conditions and people with disabilities available in church libraries. Of course, this will need continual updating, as the nature of disabling conditions is constantly redefined.

Third, consider educating congregations and parishes about people with disabilities as an ongoing part of the ministry of the church. It is far better that people ask the person with a disabling condition *about* the condition than that they spread rumors or folkloric myths about disabling conditions. Some congregations have created a committee whose primary purpose is to educate members of their church about the disabling conditions some people have.

The other untapped yet powerful source of change and support in the Church must come from those with disabling conditions themselves, along with their families and friends. The reason I have such hope in this untapped power is because of what the disability community has accomplished in the past. In developing strategies and programs among federal, state, and local governments they have secured numerous programs and golden opportunities for people with disabilities, and have had their elected representatives considering and pushing for the "equal rights" of people with disabilities in American society.

For example, one of the primary reasons that federal, state, and local governments have passed so many bills and legislative reforms for and with people with disabilities, providing so many new programs and opportunities, is because of such groups as the Association for Retarded Citizens (ARC), a group of parents of children with disabilities that began in the 1950s. Newsletters among such groups as ARC, TASH (The Association of the Severely Handicapped), and the periodical *Disability Rag* have kept people with disabilities and their families informed as to what is happening in government. It has been the parents and family members of people with disabilities who have become advocates for and with people with disabilities, who have pushed forward much-needed legislation that many thought impossible. This same "call to arms" and strategic planning and pushing is needed once again, not only within national church programs and policies, but within local churches to assure that all people, regardless of their abilities and limitations, may participate in all the facets of a church's life that make it Christ's community.

The Hopeful Results for Christ's Community

Many of the ideas suggested above work best in intentional small-or large-group, preplanned activities. Having tried some of these ideas, there are other general, overall outcomes that the congregation may arrive at. These lessons come from the work and study of Pamela Wickham-Searl, a professional special educator who has listened to the life-lessons of mothers with children with disabilities. Wickham-Searl found that many of these mothers were confronted with the sometimes flawed expertise of the "professional," who wanted to perpetuate the "deficiency" or "deviancy" model of the child with disabilities, which is *not* to the advantage of the child. What these mothers learned from this experience and, through Wickham-Searl's study, may encourage other groups and communities, is to become intense in their commitment in integrating children with disabilities in the following ways:[192]

1. **Churches will become more knowledgeable** about the disabling condition itself, and how to deal with other professionals in terms of working and living with people with disabilities. While there are (hopefully) some good, constructive ideas about what to do and how to live with people with disabilities in this book, be sure to check in with other professionals if there are any questions. In being supportive to the family as well as the friends of people with disabilities, along with the person with a disability, congregations will learn more about the various social service providers, the new skills and training, and most importantly, learn more about the person who is disabled.

2. **Churches will become more imaginative** in learning new capabilities in all the various aspects of congregational life. There is a good chance that in the context of the church, everyone will have gained some new insights into other people and the surrounding community from working and living with a person with a disability. It is important not to sequester this new insight, but to share it with others.

Throughout the teaching moments in the church's life with people with disabling conditions there will be some entertaining moments among those who participate, raising new issues and novel ideas, with the creative juices flowing and people aware, maybe for the first time, of what the world must be like for those who are disabled.

3. **Churches will become more patient and tolerant of differences** in trying to understand the life of a person with a disabling condition. The one thing that the Church has, as was shown in the life ministry of Jesus Christ, is an abundance of time to love and listen to one another.

When participating in activities that engage the imagination of many people, a bond surrounds a group as they have shared, even for just a moment, a time of laughter or pain in looking at the world through the lens of one who has a disabling condition. A teachable spirit emerges and envelops the gathering of individuals who now become a community of learners.

4. Churches will become intimate, willing to talk about the increased need for other people in supporting and caring for the person with a disability. And this works as well in the opposite direction: Become willing to receive the support and care extended to you by the person with a disabling condition.

These activities draw each person out, permitting the participant to rejoice in the life of another person that may be best revealed and understood in trying out these activities. Perhaps these stories will enable some to gain a new appreciation for how others view life. For once, there is the consideration of what the world might be like through the life experiences of those with disabilities.

5. Churches will become more resilient and not easily threatened by the new and different, finding new ways of living with others with disabilities. After a while, the congregants and parishioners will become more tolerant of the noise that some people make due to their disabling condition; they will move pews aside so that more people in stretchers and walkers may be in the church; they will slow down in reading the creeds of the Church so that the person with a learning disability can catch up and join in the responsive readings, rather than dropping out because they feel like a failure.

Once the imagination is engaged, then there is room and movement toward a many-sided conversation among those who have come to be in a church community with one another.

Keeping these five general characteristics in mind, congregations and parishes may discover what many parents with children with disabilities have found: that they are "legitimate authorities," too, with newfound abilities that they never knew they had *before* the birth or presence of someone with a disabling condition. With the presence of a person with a disabling condition, like the parents of children with disabilities, the church will also become more mature and empathetic in perceiving, in a new light, others who have certain limitations but also have a basic need to be part of Christ's community. With the inclusion of the person with a disabling condition there will emerge a collective understanding of the important perspective that people with disabilities bring to the Church. As Stanley Hauerwas writes, we need to realize that we are not members of a church as an individual matter, but as a community of Christian believers:

> We are not members of a church because we know what we believe, but we are members of a church because we need the whole church to believe for us. Often, if not most of the time, I find that I come to be part of the community that worships God not as a believer or as a faithful follower of Christ, but as someone who is just "not there." I may not be a disbeliever, but I am by no means a believer either. By being present to others in church I find I am made more than I would otherwise be—I am made one in the faith of the church. [193]

Rediscovering and Renewing the Vision of God's Banquet Feast

All of these games and activities help to create a bond among members of a church and, in the process, become the pedagogical or teaching moment in the life of a congregation or parish. The hope is that, after participating in some of the activities described throughout this chapter, both individual members and the community as a whole will begin to understand that there are some people who, because of certain physical, cognitive, mental, or sensory limitations, interact with the world differently. It is valid and essential for the health of the congregation to include the perspective of those who are disabled. Aware of the necessity of the voices or presence of those labeled "disabled" in society, conscious of the barriers that exclude many of these same people from the worshipping life of Christian communities, perhaps renewing the image of the Kingdom as God's Banquet Feast, parishes and congregations will hopefully be ready to invite, welcome, and accept all who wish to sup at God's table.

The change of heart, both among individual members and the collective gathering, emerges out of this dialogue between people concerning their experiences with one another. The line between teacher and student is blurred, if not reversed, as people become co-learners and co-participants, both learning from one another. In these activities and discussions, people have learned a great deal about their own reaction to and perception of people with disabilities. They also are open to perceiving the world anew when looking through the experiences of those with disabling conditions. The true teachers in this setting are often those people with disabling conditions who become the instructors, through experience, for the able-bodied learners.[194]

For the person who is able bodied, considering what the world is like from the vantage point of the person with a disabling condition affirms that person's existence and the existence of the one who is nondisabled. The humanity of both groups of people is affirmed. To engage in a relationship with and treat one who has a disabling condition as a valid and valuable member of God's community, to be challenged and changed by this relationship, is to truly *be with* another person. In this process of *being with* the other person, God's Spirit emerges and embraces the two. This is not a relationship of mindless chatter but of true dialogue as perceptions of God shared between two people in the context of a Christian community who worships together, learns together, and prays together.

The active inclusion of people with disabling conditions, like Annie, Rose, and Sue from the above stories, is long overdue. The need is urgent and pressing upon congregations and parishes. In participating in and experiencing some of these activities, both among those who are able bodied and those who are disabled begin to come together around the Lord's table, where Holy Communion is shared, more ready to learn from each other's experiences in life. In the next chapter, the task is to think of creative ways of bringing together those who are abled bodied with those with certain limited abilities in order that there is much good table talk among others around God's Banquet Feast on earth.

6

◆ ◆ ◆

The Banquet Feast:
Christian Religious Education
with People with Disabilities

I n the book *After Virtue*, the philosopher Alisdair MacIntyre writes
that one thing we can predict is the "permanent unpredictability of
human life."[195] The idea that we can predict what another human
being is going to do in the future, that we can somehow control and
manage a person's character, words, actions, thoughts, and feelings, is
an illusion fostered by the social scientific tradition. MacIntyre argues
that all we can predict is that human beings are unpredictable because
we live in a now-unpredictable social world.[196]

In welcoming people with disabling conditions into Christ's community, Christians welcome some people whose actions and behaviors are
unpredictable, to say the least. Yet in welcoming these brothers and
sisters, the Christian community becomes a place that is made up of
people in all their richness and weakness, abilities and limitations.
The Church becomes a place that learns to accept people who can be
themselves in front of one another, and therefore may forgive each
other as people learn to be vulnerable in a welcoming spirit.[197]

This spirit of welcome is essential for the spiritual well-being of
Christian communities, for in the act of inviting the stranger, the one
who disturbs us, God brings a gift through the "unexpected" guest who
causes a community to grow both in size and in depth in truly knowing

God.[198] Learning to open our hearts to people with disabilities is bound to be painful as it will call the able-bodied person to struggle with his or her woundedness. Welcoming anyone, regardless of how able or disabled they may appear, is a risky and unpredictable enterprise, yet vital for the health of Christ's body.

In this next section, there are two stories that reveal the unpredictable nature of people with disabilities, and the gift that this quality of life brings to the Christian community's understanding of human nature and God.

Welcoming the Unpredictable

This theme of unpredictability has repeated itself time and again in my life experiences with people who are disabled, especially those who are mentally retarded. Once I think I have figured out how someone is going to respond to a preplanned experience, I am continually amazed at how much I am off the mark. For example, consider Sal. Sal is a hugger. She will, if given a chance, throw herself on you, with all her 80 pounds of freckles, strawberry-blonde hair, and childhood kinetic energy, as she simultaneously asks *whether* she can hug you. Sal is mentally retarded and hyperactive (Attention Deficit/Hyperactivity Disorder); she also has a speech impediment.

In working with Sal there have been a lot of surprises. She has been living in an institution for over two years. After being with her for a few weeks, during a time when I had been teaching the young people on the unit songs and Bible stories, Sal eagerly joined in the singing and stories, sitting close to me and touching the guitar, feeling the vibration through the wooden panels. Just the other day, when I started to sing "Jesus Loves Me," Sal suddenly sat straight up, started bouncing up and down, and raised both hands high over her head. "I know that song," she said. "Start it again," she squealed in her delight at knowing the song. And singing it again, Sal revealed for the whole circle that she knew the hand signs for the entire song. We were all amazed, staff and children alike. What is remarkable is that she had to have learned this song before she came to the hospital, because her speech pathologist hadn't taught her the hand gestures, nor had I; and she had never sung that song for us before. For over two years, Sal has know that song far better than we could have imagined, could have thought . . .

well, possible. Finishing her encore with a big, knowing grin, she said "I love that song. It's one of my favorites. Can we sing it again?"

What happened? The unpredictable human being and the even more unpredictable God changed how I experienced the song "Jesus Loves Me." It was as if, with the wave of her hands, a doorway opened, and Sal and the rest of the group could truly meet on common ground and communicate with each other. Her knowledge of the song and accompanying hand gestures became a common link by which we could communicate with one another and both learn something new about each other and God. Indeed, Sal's hand gestures transformed my understanding of the song and of Sal herself.[199]

Another spontaneous teaching moment, where the unpredictability of human nature was once again revealed, occurred in my relationship with Randy, a young boy who is 13 years old and has an emotional disability. One day, out of the blue, Randy asked me if I would read a long story with him, *Joseph and the Coat of Many Colors.*[200] What is intriguing about Randy's own narrative is what he has discovered in this biblical story: Randy has found some similar themes from his life in Joseph's adventures. Randy has come to see that both he and Joseph had once lived in a loving family, and then they were without the support of this love, and finally, in God, they found the support and love to get on with life's adventures.

Randy sought me out when it came close to the Jewish Passover days. Before Randy was placed into institutional life, he had lived in Michigan as well as in southern Florida, with a father who was Jewish and a mother who was Roman Catholic. Since then, the parents have separated and divorced, and all the family that Randy has now is his sister and brother-in-law. He expressed real interest in undoing some confusion that he felt in trying to decide if he was either Jewish or Christian, and he really wanted to figure out what he believed, and where he should go to find God.

In the following month, Randy asked me to begin reading the story of Joseph with him while he was at the hospital. He had heard and read the story in the Bible before, but this book gave a little more detail as a fictional retelling. Off we went to the lakeside by his unit to sit on the dock and read the book together. He would read one page, and I would read the next. His tongue tripped over many of the words, due to a reading disability, but he tried his best to make sense of them. We had a vow that we would read one chapter a week, or thereabouts, until we finished the book, and then we would find another book to read.

After we read the beginning chapter, Randy thanked me for the time we sat and read together. He said that he had had many dreams in his life, too, just like Joseph. Once, he dreamt of God talking to him while he was laying in bed, and God said that he loved Randy, which meant a great deal to him as he often didn't feel loved. Randy continued, saying that most of the time his dreams barely begin before he wakes up suddenly, and then he can't remember what he was dreaming, which frustrates him to no end. Yet sometimes after this happens, he begins to dream an entirely new dream the next time he dozes off to sleep.

During our next reading time, the story of Joseph focused on the promises and lies people tell one another. In the Joseph story, Joseph is given rank within the household of Potiphar because he tells the truth, and uses his new position wisely. However, the other slaves are not happy about this promotion of Joseph in the royal court, and they conspire against Joseph and lie about him, accusing him of cheating and stealing from Potiphar.

After reading this part of the story, Randy turned to me and said that he knew that it was better to tell the truth than to lie, "because when you lie, the truth comes back to haunt you." Sometimes, Randy has agreed with his peers to tell a lie, or won't snitch on someone to the staff of the hospital, but still the truth comes out. Randy said that the lesson is easier to hear, but harder to live out: Always tell the truth, and keep your promises.[201]

Unfolding Our Stories in God's Story of Love

Trying as hard as we can to create labels and categories, goals and learning objectives for those we call "disabled," trying to be a culture of Christian care that will stimulate the senses and encourage learning, so much of the "good" done in the names of special education and Christian religious education occurs *in spite of* our good work. Granted, sometimes people learn what Christian religious educators want them to learn through the methods and processes that have been developed. However, it is amazing how often, in the midst of human relationships, established and maintained within the specific context of the Christian community, it is the unpredictable nature of God that transforms lives.

God's presence is evident in the life stories of Sal and Randy. What is unique about these stories is that none of the labels attached to Sal and Randy really told us much about these two people and their relationship with God. These labels often play an important part if one is trying to make a general, overall sketch of certain characteristics that people with specific disabling conditions have in common in a narrowly defined context, like a special education classroom or a hospital unit. However, when trying to engage in an educating moment with another person in the Christian community, suddenly, spontaneity and a sense of adventure are the rule of the day, and the labels and categories are of little, if any, help. As the educational theoretician and kindergarten teacher Vivian Gussin Paley has written, we can be known only in the "unfolding of our unique stories within the context of everyday events.[202]

Having prepared the congregation and parish for the presence of people with disabilities in the Church in general, and the Christian religious education context in particular, this chapter's focus is on Christian religious education with people with disabling conditions. Christian religious education with people with disabilities in the traditional church-based education program is going to be more complicated and challenging because the theories of Christian religious education have been constructed, in large part, *without* people with disabling conditions in mind.

There are two different approaches to this work. The first is the traditional, able-bodied-centered, integrated model that assumes that the curriculum is based on the public-school paradigm of doing education. It borrows heavily from the field of special education and psychology. The practical activities discussed are basic adaptations that the Christian religious educator may use in helping the person with a disabling condition to become a more active participant in the current programs and Christian religious education activities for normal, able-bodied people. The goal of these adaptations is to help fit the person with a disabling condition into the "normal," able-bodied Christian religious education programs and activities. Integration or mainstreaming people with disabling conditions into active contact with non-exceptional children and adults in a church is achieved when the one with a disability can join in the activities of those who are "able-bodied."[203]

For example, in the preceding stories, what would be important is helping Sal to communicate her love of Jesus not only by hand gestures, which, in and of themselves are a strong witness to God's Spirit at work, but also by verbal or linguistic means according to some curriculum guide put out by a mainline, denominational office. This is because verbal or linguistic method of communication, which is often not considered by some a gestureful manner of communication, is what is normal for most people in our congregations and parishes. For Randy, the place to resolve his identity issues would be perhaps in a pastoral counseling session, with the goal of enabling him to find his identity by putting his story in the context of God's story.

The second approach is based on the paradigmatic story of the Banquet Feast. The goal of Christian religious education is one of inclusion, where we take seriously the experiences and perspective of all God's children, including those with disabilities. We consider the way each of us imagines God. It is an approach that respects how each person in Christ's community understand's his or her story of life in the midst of God's sacred story.

The emphasis of this approach is on doing Christian religious education *with* people who also happen to be disabled, by focusing on certain gestures: listening to their stories, worshiping with them, dancing with them, playing music with them, admiring their artwork. Rather than making those with disabilities express their image of God Christian faith in primarily a linguistic or verbal mode just like "us," the focus is shifted to encouraging both the able-bodied Christian religious educator and other participants to learn the logic, the grammar, the artistic mode of communication best suited for the person with a disabling condition via gestures.

My hope is that churches will come to recognize the untapped yet vital ministry with and by those who have certain limitations and abilities quite unlike anyone else in the world. This second approach is harder to practice and will take longer to accomplish, and it may seem strange and silly at certain moments. It is hard to dance out the movement of the Holy Spirit in one's life with someone who is labeled "severely mentally retarded" if the Christian religious educator doesn't like to dance. It will be different to do a lesson completely through drawing pictures rather than talking. It will be unique to say unison prayers like the Lord's Prayer slowly so that the person with dyslexia may join in. It will be unique to worship with someone in a hospital stretcher or with someone who has Tourette's syndrome and is making involuntary noises throughout worship. Again, as Stanley Hauerwas reminds, us, it is exactly to the extent that those with disabilities create the unexpected that they remind us that God is not to be domesticated: "In worship the church is made vulnerable to a God that would rule this world not by coercion, but through the unpredictability of love.[204] It means letting go of the pretensions of the able-bodied community, letting go of power, in order to finally gain an appreciation for those with disabling conditions and how *we* perceive God, the world around *us*, and the love of God extended to all of *us*.

A Mainstreaming Approach to Christian Religious Education

This section will briefly cover some pragmatic adaptations for people with disabling conditions that may be used in current Christian religious education programs in congregations and parishes. The goal of the Christian religious education program that uses these adaptive ideas is to work toward normalization of programs or least restrictive activities for all participants in the activities. By providing normalizing and least-restrictive activities, those with disabilities will be mainstreamed—the process of bringing people with disabling conditions into contact with those who are able bodied in a religious education activity.[205]

The basic assumptions for this normalization or mainstreaming approach are:

First, that Christian religious education programs are not the place to conduct or carry out any assessments as to the labeling or categorization of children and adults who are disabled. Most likely, this work has been conducted within other, more appropriate centers that focus on assessments and diagnostic activities that will lead toward the necessary educational, medical, and therapeutic programs or activities. Knowledge of the educational, medical, and therapeutic needs may be helpful at some moments in the Christian's religious education program.

Second, this section assumes that the goal is total integration of children and adults with disabling conditions into the normal program of Christian religious education activities in the Christian community. There is too much research in special education and psychology that shows that children with disabling conditions, like mental retardation, hearing and visual impairments, and physical disabilities, are motivated to perform and stretch beyond themselves physically, socially, and educationally when participating in activities *with* children who are able bodied.[206]

Third, even though there are few programs written for the active inclusion of people with various disabling conditions in the Christian religious education curriculum, it is important to include activities throughout the year where it is natural to integrate and include those with disabling conditions without special adaptations. Many times, people with disabling conditions get tired of feeling like something special is being done *for* them and *to* them. It is helpful to include activities in a religious education program where people can share their thoughts and feelings out of their abilities without any special adaptations. In other words, work towards making everyone feel like a part of the community, not special and exceptional.

Fourth, try not to ignore or overly praise the child or adult with a disabling condition. Remember, those with disabling conditions are *people first*, human beings who have thoughts and feelings and a variety of potential abilities and disabilities. While many labels and categories give the Christian religious educator some perspective on what a person can do, the label does not adequately explain their character or who they are. As the anthropologist Richard Katz wrote, labels hide rather than reveal the person: "They dramatize to the point of caricature, distancing us from others so that we need not relate to them."[207]

Fifth, ask the parents, guardians, or family members of children with disabilities, or ask young adults and adults directly, what they can do. This is widely overlooked in some congregations and parishes, even though one of the key reasons that people with disabilities have not been welcomed into the Church is because members don't know what to do with the person with a disability. What the natural community surrounding the person with a disability will tell the church are the nuances and intricacies of abilities and limitations. By following a learning pattern established in school, in the workplace, or at home, members of the church become part of an overall program of providing the least restrictive environment for people with disabilities, rather than being one more hurdle for people with disabilities to jump over. For those who are more restricted in their abilities, when a church continues a plan established in these other areas of a person's life, they are reinforcing a program rather than the more detrimental act of ignoring an already established helpful process.

Finally, be sure that the Christian religious education activity takes place in a physical space that conveys love and acceptance. In special education terms, create a place and activities that are largely non-threatening and more or less success-oriented at first. Since much that goes on in churches bring both moments of comfort as well as discomfort, try to shape a place and activities where people are truly learning to dialogue with one another, and in the discourse able to accept, love, and celebrate the diversity and uniqueness of each member of the community. Both people with disabling conditions and the able-bodied members are looking for the warm embrace of Christ's community in order to continue their journey of Christian faith. Encourage a mixture of activities that highlight our individual uniqueness as well as activities that celebrate our common dependence on one another in community and in God. Help make the space where Christian religious education "happens" be a place where all feel welcomed, loved, and nurtured by God's spirit and love.

What follows are some activities and changes in the environment that will encourage learning and integration in the religious education programs in communities of faith. The categories will be used with the descriptions found of disabling conditions in Chapter 2 of this book.

Mental Retardation

1. With children and adults who are mentally retarded, one of the best ways to help them feel at home is through the very structure of the program. Follow a ritual, a basic structured format in religious education activities every time that you meet, as participants will feel most comfortable with a familiar sequence of activities.

2. Use words and language they can understand, and be sure to define and describe new concepts and terms in concrete, tangible expressions. "Keep it simple" will work a lot of the time, though it is important to respect each individual, especially when you find out that their vocabulary may be broader than first anticipated.

3. Use a friendship or buddy system in some activities, depending solely on the needs of the person with a disabling condition. This is important not only for those who are mentally retarded, but for the members who are able bodied as well. After a few activities, see where the friendship patterns develop and encourage everyone in a class, both those who are mentally retarded and those who are able-bodied, to find partners. Be sure that those who are mentally retarded are partnered with those who are able bodied for these activities. However, there will be some people who don't need and don't want a special "buddy."

4. In the activities of a Christian religious education program, be sure that, as educators, you have broken down the lesson to their most basic level so that the child or adult with mental retardation may understand what is happening and can participate in the activities.

5. Feel free to use many concrete, tangible objects in working through a lesson in a Christian religious education activity with children and adults who are mentally retarded. Engage their imagination, along with the rest of the group, by using projects and lessons that use, for example, art, music, dance, and drama. For example, try teaching lessons using clay, flannel-board objects, music instruments, construction paper cut-outs, costumes, masks, and role playing the biblical stories.

6. When using a Bible, maybe try using a children's Bible, like the *Taizé Bible*. Many of these Bibles are full of pictures and are updated versions of the stories in language that is more easily comprehended by the child or adult with mental retardation.

7. Be prepared for the unexpected. Some people with mental retardation may turn in a messy art project, while others turn in art projects that are beautiful and inspiring. Each one has his or her own way of expressing ideas about God and life.

Learning Disabilities
1. Be prepared for various levels of functioning when pursuing activities that involve writing and reading in the Christian religious educational programs. Some people with learning disabilities will take

longer to read or write during an activity. In some cases, you may want someone to read a story out loud rather than having a group read a story in silence. Sometimes the user of a computer in the classroom with whole words on the monitor can help the child or adult with a learning disability participate in the activity if writing and reading are part of the lesson plan.

2. Use rituals in the Christian religious education program. Be sure that the rituals are repeated each time that the child or adult with a learning disability participants in the activities.

3. A buddy or partner system will work well with some children who have a learning disability. Be sure that many of the activities that are pursued in the religious education program are done in partnerships.

4. Some children with learning disabilities may act out, displaying behaviors that are inappropriate because they feel uncomfortable in not being able to follow an activity. Be sure to go over the lesson plans or the directions for a project until *everyone* understands what they are to do. Some people with learning disabilities may need to really focus and physically see eye to eye with the Christian religious educator in order to understand what is being said.

Communication and Language Disorders

1. Listen to *what* the child or adult is saying rather than focusing on *how* they are saying it. The role and function of the Christian religious educator is not to be the speech therapist.[208]

2. On the one hand, let those with the communication disorder talk when they want to rather than forcing them to communicate in a social setting. Many people with communication disorders feel embarrassed about the way that they talk.

3. On the other hand, be sure to solicit the opinion of those who have a communication disorder. While they may have a difficult time talking, this does not mean that they do not have thoughts or feelings about what is being discussed in a religious education activity.

4. Use concrete, tangible objects when conducting lessons. Use

flannel-board images, pictures, cut-outs, and any other images when conducting activities.

5. Some people with communication disorders may need the help of an electronic keyboard, a computer, or a language board. This is especially true of some people with cerebral palsy, and some people with autistic behavior. Be patient with this mode of communication, and help others learn how to communicate with those who need such adaptive equipment.

Hearing Impairment

1. In most cases, it is vital and helpful to find out which method of communication is being used by the person with a hearing loss. Some will use oral communication, others cued speech, while many will use American Sign Language. Identify which method of communication is the preference of the child. Then the task of the religious educator is to either learn how to use this method in teaching, or to find someone else to translate the lesson.

2. Use visual images to communicate ideas, stories, and lessons. Again, concrete images and tasks that use clay, pictures, overheads, and other visual adaptations will aid the person with a hearing loss.

3. Try to focus and limit the amount of loudness of sound in a room. It is often hard for a person with a hearing impairment to focus on one sound or voice in a room full of people talking. If there are many sounds, many people with hearing losses are confused and lost in what is happening.

4. Use movement and dance in many of the lessons. The use of some pantomime is appropriate and engaging not only for the person with a hearing loss but also for one who is able bodied.

5. Many who have a hearing loss are able to read lips and may have some residual hearing. If this is the case, be sure that the person who has a hearing impairment can see the face of the religious educator rather than sitting behind or on the side of the educator.

Visual Impairment

1. In the room where the religious education activity is being held, be sure the setup stays as consistent as possible. People with visual

impairments become accustomed to the room setup and can negotiate it once they have committed it to memory.

2. Be prepared for some mannerisms that provide some stimulation for people with visual impairments. Some people will rock in place or pat toys or other objects, others will look off in the distance away from the speaker, while many will rub their closed eyes.

3. When using objects in a lesson or activity, let the person with a visual impairment hold and touch the object. Depending on the amount of vision, some will hold it close to their eyes, while others will use other senses like touch, motion, and smell to find out about what they are holding.

For some people with visual impairments, if they want to know how you feel, touch is the best method of communication. With permission of the person with a visual impairment, you may want to pat a shoulder or give a hug while telling why.

4. People with visual impairments, though they are not deaf, appreciate it if you talk to them rather than away from them. Raising one's voice, however, does not help.

5. Give people with visual impairments time to move and acquaint themselves with physical action if this is called for in an activity. Sometimes, a buddy or partner system is organized so that there will be someone else to guide the person with a visual impairment. Let the buddy or partner guide, not lead, the individual with a visual impairment, avoiding pushing or cajoling. This is best done by letting the person with a visual impairment hold onto the arm of the sighted person.

6. When talking about an activity in one part of a room, don't use words like "this" or "over there." Be as precise as possible in using language, telling the person with a visual impairment exactly where they should go and what they should be doing.

7. Try to use Bibles, hymn books, prayer books, bulletins, song books, and newsletters in either Braille or large print.

Behavioral Problems

1. One of the best ways of maintaining order is by keeping all of one's senses busy and stimulated. Keep someone with a behavioral problem active in a project with others in a small-group setting.

2. Sometimes, it may be best for the Christian religious educator or an assistant to work one-on-one with a person with a behavioral problem, perhaps helping him or her work on reading or writing during an activity.

3. In the Christian religious education activity, be sure that you follow a similar pattern or ritual so that one knows what to expect next.

4. Ask the person with a behavioral problem their thoughts and feelings in religious education activities. Often what a person with a behavioral problem desires is to be heard and accepted by others in a peer group.

Multiple and Severe Disabilities
1. It is best to truly know the functional abilities of this person. Ask the person with multiple and severe disabilities, or in some cases the person's friends, what they can and like to do.

2. Try to always plan activities where all may join in, including the person with multiple and severe disabilities. In singing, playing games, reading and writing, and participating in group learning activities, find ways with the person who is disabled to enable them to be active participants.

3. Be sure there is enough space so that a person using a wheelchair, hearing aids or communication boards can easily maneuver.

4. When needed, be sure that the person with multiple disabilities can be with a partner or a buddy to provide aid when asked for in the activity.

Physical Disabilities
1. Get to know what the person with a physical disability feels comfortable doing in a group, especially when pursuing an active game. Find ways of adapting activities to include the person with certain physical limitations.

2. Avoid smothering the person with a physical disability with attention, but give assistance when needed—for instance, in eating some

foods or in unwrapping a straw. Again, the partner or buddy system works well with many who have a physical disability.

3. Talk directly to a person with a physical disability. Try to be on the same eye level when conversing with a person in a wheelchair.

Health Impairments

It is important to know when a child or an adult has a specific health impairment for some activities within a Christian religious education program. For example, when going on a weekend adventure, be sure you know who has special medications to take, who has to limit physically strenuous activities, and who needs to take other precautions need to be considered. It is also helpful to tell the person responsible in a Christian religious education program who has a heart condition or what to do if someone has an epileptic seizure.

Christian Religious Education with People With Disabilities

The previous section covered some of the "tricks" of the special educator, therapist, and psychologist in making adaptations in curriculum and the environment to develop a context of Christian religious education.

Another approach to Christian religious education and people with disabilities is one based more on an inclusive community of Christ: Christian religious education begins with *being with* people with disabilities in a common space and place and time, This fits with the metaphor of God's Banquet Feast and the notion of dining together.

For example, people come to dinner and eat food because of the biological necessity, and also to fulfill the most individual of needs: becoming and creating a community.[209] Like the guests at a banquet feast, Christians come together into community because there is *nothing* anywhere else that is capable of bonding willful, broken human selves except God, who leads all people into the heart of forgiveness.[210] Christian religious education involves inviting, welcoming, and most importantly, *being with* each other in a common place, because all Christians have a common need to know and be known by God.[211]

One place that this transcendent yet immediate knowing of God happens is in the context of relationships with others in Christ's community. Yet to relate with those members with disabilities, sometimes the key is not for them to speak the language or picture the world and God in the same way as the person who is able-bodied. Again, suffering occurs when there is an attempt in making "them" like "us."

This relationship also occurs when the person who is able-bodied tries to gain some understanding of the world and God through the perspective of one who is labeled "disabled." Learning about the world and God's Story through the perspective of one who is disabled will involve being challenged to use our creative imagination and the tools of art, dance, music, and drama; as well as the written and spoken word; as we learn to participate in Christian religious education *with* a person with a disability.

The key to this approach is to use our creative imagination in the context of the Christian community. Being created human, we all have the God-given, human characteristic of imagination. Imagination is what we share in common. And it is through the use of our collective imagination that we will be able to discover our place around the common table of God's Banquet Feast.

In this section, the various parts of a more integrated approach to Christian religious education, with people with disabilities along with those who are able-bodied, will be discussed as prelude to gestures in Chapter 7. Key to this common language between those with disabilities and those who are non-disabled. Second, the imagination in Christian religious education that depends heavily upon the use of rituals and the creative arts as a way of placing our life stories in the context of God's sacred story. Third, our creative imaginations that enable us to learn from one another about the Christian life as we share our stories in the larger context of God's sacred story, which is celebrated in the rituals of the Church. For it is in Christ's community where we will learn many gestures that aid us all in understanding the wondrous things of God in Christ who is *the* Host at this miraculous and sumptuous Banquet Feast of love.

Imagination: What Is It?

Imagination: It's something that we all possess as human beings. In Genesis 1:27, we read that human beings were created in the "image of God."[212] The Old Testament theologian Walter Brueggemann wrote that being created in the image of God, human beings were created with the gift and ability to be creative. Creativity requires imagination, to envision what we want to create or craft and to dream about new possibilities.[213] It is this ability to imagine that has led to some of humankind's greatest creative moments, expressed in art, music, drama, dance, and inventions of all kinds.

Imagination is the capacity not only to see the world and others around us in a new light, but to look beyond things as they are and to see them through a new perspective or someone else's eyes. It is the power that enables us to perceive the normal in the abnormal, to perceive the cosmos in the midst of chaos.[214] Imagination makes it possible for us to envision *who* God is in our lives, *what* God's story is all about for the Christian community, and *how* we are embedded in and surrounded by God's love. To quote the writer of the book of Hebrews, though faith is the "assurance of things hoped for, the conviction of things not seen" (Hebrews 11:1, NRSV), it is finally our capacity to imagine that enables all of the members of God's community to vividly envision such a loving God who brings hope, justice, care, comfort, and love to all who believe in such Good News. The playwright George Bernard Shaw wrote in his play on the life of Joan of Arc, that God communicates with human beings through the use of imagination:

> "I hear voices telling me what to do," says St. Joan in Shaw's play; "they come from God." "They come from your imagination," replied Robert De Baudricort. "Of course, that is how the messages of God come to us."[215]

Even in the talk of banquet feast there is not only the pleasure of eating, "the room in which the dinner is served, the tables and chairs, the lights, the decorations, and the companions themselves, is a common *image* for the cosmos, for life, or for Paradise."[216] Imagination is central in some Christian poetry that makes Paradise a banquet, especially a wedding dinner, "with death a solemn but triumphant procession into the dining hall, beyond the threshold of which lies bliss for the soul as bride of the Beloved."[217]

Imagination and People with Disabilities

In working with many people who are disabled, including those who are labeled "autistic" or "severely mentally retarded," the one common characteristic is the use of imagination. For example, in the above story we see Sal's imagination at work in not only reconstructing from her memory the hand gestures she once knew to the song "Jesus Loves Me," but now using the beauty of the hand gestures to the same song sung by others in the hospital. Randy used his imagination to understand that his story and Joseph's story have many themes in common. By placing his story of life into Joseph's story, Randy has found that God's love extends to him, even in the remote wildness of a secular hospital. Using his imagination, Randy even drew his own idea of what Joseph's coat of many colors looked like.

In reflecting upon these creative, imaginative responses to this project, there are some general observations:

First, all of these children with disabilities live, like the rest of us, in a *qualitative* world. By "qualitative," I mean we live in a world consisting of qualities we are able to experience like color, texture, smell, sounds, and motion. All of these elements permeate and effect our very lives. We become so conscious and dependent on these qualitative aspects of this world that we begin to express ourselves with others through specific modes that incorporate and stimulate certain senses, as the artist communicates through art and the writer communicates through words.

Second, not only do the senses capture the qualitative world for just the moment, but within the mind, the sense of this qualitative world reside. All people are able to remember or recall, in concrete terms, what was going on in their world; their mind's eye captured some tangible fragments of what was happening around them.

For example, Sal remembered the hand signs that had been used years before when she would go to church with her family. Randy had already imagined what the coat was like that Joseph was wearing.

Third, given the right tools, the correct vehicles, the perfect music instrument, the appropriate pens, crayon and paper, people with disabling conditions can make public what is private. In other words, the creative arts may become the primary means and ways of communicating with each other. What was demonstrated in the above stories with Sal's hand gestures and songs, and Randy's stories and pictures, was the creative use of objects in expressing one's self in the learning relationship.

The educator Elliot Eisner calls these creative ways and means "forms of representation," which are necessary in making what is a private imaginative perception public.[218] These forms of representation are the pictures, speech, dance, bodily gestures, numbers, visual art, music, computer graphics, songs, and physical touch, to name a few, that become devices that enable us to share our internal, private world. These forms of representation provide a concrete, qualitative pathway toward filling our mind with ideas and impressions. We learn best when we truly experience, firsthand, what the educator wants us to learn.

What has been at work in the lives of these people labeled "mentally retarded" or "emotionally disabled" is what works within all of us: imagination. Imagination is universal in that we all have it and, given the right circumstances, can express it in the public realm, in our congregations and parishes. Imagination is the common thread uniting all of us, regardless of our I.Q. score, our emotional profile, our physical limitation, or our social adaptive behavior. We need our imaginations in order to reconstruct the past, understand the present, and dream about the future. Our imagination is at work at this very moment, in our relationships with one another. Imagination is what finally provides the common ground experiences where those who are labeled "disabled" and those who are "able bodied" can meet and be with one another in Christian religious education activities.

The Importance of Imagination in the Rituals in Christian Religious Education

An important part of Christian religious education with people with disabilities in community with those who are able-bodied are gesture-ful rituals. Rituals are important in both banquets and in Christian worship. For example, during meals and in worship, rituals serve the role of setting expectations for the participants, providing a guide to the process of eating and worshipping, and keeping things going when our energy has diminished. In setting the expectations, the constancy of rituals enables those who are eating to concentrate not on what is going on with the meal and worship, but on the messages embodied in the discussions among those gathered to eat or to pray.[219]

Rituals are also an expression of solidarity with one another. Table manners and rituals in the Church dictate the way in which it is commonly agreed that eating and worshipping *should be* performed. This theme of commonality and solidarity nurtured in rituals is echoed in the writing of the anthropologist Victor Turner who wrote that rituals are necessary in community life providing a sense of security, cohesion, meaning, purpose, and aim for life.[220]

For many people with disabilities, the rituals of the Church during worship, as well as the rituals in our Christian religious education program, not only provide the structure we all need to experience God. More importantly, they foster solidarity among the disabled, the non-disabled, and God in Christ. The use of symbols like the sacraments, and narrative symbols like the reading and acting out of Bible stories, sets the stage for experiences of God. For it is the experience of God in Christ that is essential for the Christian community. And it is our many experiences of God that gives rise to theological thought: Christianity's conceptualizations of God in Christ are grounded in the community's imaginative, intimate, and intuitive knowledge of God.[221]

The Primacy of Community in Christian Religious Education

In discussing Christian religious education in a congregation or parish with people who are able bodied and disabled, it is important to understand that religious education is an act of the entire Christian community, and not separate from it. Christians have no identity outside of the Christian community, and without identity, we know neither who we are nor to whom we belong. The greatness of community is that it provides us with the essential context for all of life; it nurtures and shapes our lives that are touched by many others, fostering great compassion and awareness of both the abilities and limitations of human community, and God's love for creation.[222]

The Christian community can learn much from this image of a banquet feast as there are similarities between both. For example, like the church, banquets are collective ceremonies, a time above all others when individuals learn to share pleasures and to heighten the sense of pleasure with one another in talking and being together.[223] As collective ceremonies, banquets become places of celebration of the relationships among the diners; and expressions of order, knowledge, competence, sympathy, and consensus about important aspects of the world; and sources of support for the group of invited guests.[224] Feasts display the fruits of human labor and good fortune among all people. Like a banquet feast, congregants and parishioners come together to celebrate their relationship, based upon not only their love for each other, but their love of God, who loved us first. Based on God's love, Christians structure their time and place by a certain order, fostering certain knowledge and competence, and supporting one another as fellow guests.

This understanding of community is fundamental, for Christian religious education requires "participating in a community through which our lives are constituted by a unity more profound than our individual needs."[225] One cannot teach or instruct others in the content of the Christian faith separate from any determinative practices of the Christian community; "to be a Christian is more than to understand this or that doctrine."[226] Again, as the theologian Stanley Hauerwas writes, there are times when Christians are just "not there" in Christ; we need the whole church to believe *for* us. By being present to others in church, we find the strength to be more than we would be otherwise as we are made one in the faith of the church.[227]

Hauerwas continues, reminding us that the condition of people with disabilities, especially those with developmental disabilities, is the condition of us all "insofar as we are faithful followers of Christ":

> The church is not a collection of individuals but rather a people on a journey who are known by the time they take to help one another along the way. The mentally handicapped constitute such time as we know that God would not have us try to make the world better if that means leaving them behind. They are the way we must learn to walk in the journey that God has given us called kingdom. They are God's imagination and to the extent we become one with them, we become God's imagination for the world.[228]

The Centrality of God's Story in the Christian Community

What is holding the Christian community together, determining its course, and exciting its collective imagination is God's sacred story: the Bible.

The idea of being fed and living off of God's Word and story as part of the education of Christians was taken not only figuratively but literally in many early monastic communities: Meals were accompanied by the reading of the Holy Scripture, the auditory memory absorbed textual sequences while the body took in its nourishment:

> The ambiguous meaning of the word *collation* in the language of monks is very significant: the term denotes a sermon given after a meal, but also the meal itself, as if listening and eating, discourse and digestion were identical operations.[229]

The Renaissance scholar Michel Jeanneret continues, writing that "the reception of books and ingestion of food were often linked. Food for the mind and food for the body, absorbed and digested together, joined in a single physiological experience.[230]

Jeanneret also cites the work of the Church Father, Erasmus, who wrote of ways of finding a balanced state of well-being in which the body and spirit are equally fulfilled in a climate of human warmth in a Godly Feast:

> The friends retreat to a country house . . . and celebrate a frugal meal in imitation of the Last Supper. The spirit of the Gospel, the concern for purity and for remaining faithful to the lesson of Christ dominate the gathering. The real food is God's word, and true pleasure lies in the interpretation of the biblical message. The natural setting and eating well are seen as mere symbols; everything culminates in communion in the divine mystery.[231]

Not only are communion meals held together and people fed and sustained by stories of God, but, as the novelist Barry Lopez is correct in stating, "*everything* is held together with stories . . . that is all that is holding us together, stories and compassion.[232] This is exactly what holds the Church together—the ongoing master or sacred story of God's love for creation. We can only know ourselves and one another by the unfolding of our unique stories in the context of the Christian community that shares in common the telling, retelling, and ritualistic celebration of God's story. For it is God's story that precedes our very birth and entrance into the midst of the Christian community that holds the responsibility of sharing the story, and is made richer by our addition and contribution in the life of the Church.

In Christian religious education it needs to be understood that each person has his or her own story of love and despair, of our shifting through our family's and church's dirt and moments of glory, of being part of a motley gathering of human hearts who have a clean and piercing longing for God's story that is spiritually significant in the mundane affairs of the human life.[233] The collective imagination of our hearts and minds empowers each one of us to finally gain some understanding of how someone else perceives the world and God, thus allowing us to begin learning from one another and from God.

The Role of the Christian Religious Educator

The role of the Christian religious educator is to be the Host who invites and waits for the guest, the learner, to come to the banquet feast, the Christian community. As the host of the banquet of learning, the host is responsible for the guest within the boundaries of his or her domain. In the case of Christian religious education, the educator, be it an individual or the congregation as a whole, is responsible for the nurturing of the guest, the learners, in the context of the Christian community.

Like a host at a banquet, the Christian religious educator extends the invitation to come and be part of a supportive, loving, compassionate relationship to many guests who may share their lives and ideas about God. What the Christian religious educator does is draw lines—not between the students and the educator only, but one that connects the individuals and their images of God to God's story of love that was first learned in their churches. The educator hopes to find a way of evoking the students' images, vision, or observations and understandings of the world we live in every day with the help of God's love.

For example, in Sal's story, I was not aware that, underneath the frenetic energy, there was a measure of great learning and remembering going on in her life as she brought back from her memory the hand gestures to "Jesus Loves Me." For Randy, I was surprised by his request to tell his story, which enabled me to invite him to learn more about story of life in the context of God's story. Once the invitation was accepted, I was able, with each person's permission, to make a personal connection. And I have truly been changed by my relationship with these two as they became my Christian religious educators and I became their student.

The Role of the Learner

The role of the learner is often as guest. As the guest, the learner is there to receive and show support and love, and to renew neighborly bond with the host.[234]

What is interesting about the relationship between a host and guest is that there is a decided imbalance in the relationship, with the purpose of bringing about reciprocity or equalization that is forbidden at present, but will be achieved later on.[235] In other words, there is going to be a reversal in roles, where the guest will become host, and the host will become the guest at another, later time.[236]

Sal was not only open to receiving the invitation to join in the song, but she taught the educator about what she knew. Randy was not only eager to know more about Joseph, but also to share what he thought was important in Joseph's and Randy's narratives.

The dialogue between host and guest, educator and student, is embedded and takes place in the context of the Christian community. What is uncovered and revealed is due not only to the bond that developed between two people who care for one another, but also to God's Spirit working within the context of the Christian community. It is out of our relationship with God's love that lives are touched and what could have been babbling becomes true, meaningful dialogue and revelation of God.[237]

Our human imagination, which is given expression and made public through creative forms of representation, is a powerful way that those who are able bodied and disabled may learn to share, metaphorically speaking, their stories with one another. It is in the sharing of stories, both human and sacred, that our faith, and our knowledge of God, is shaped and nurtured and we discover identity and belonging in the midst of God's love.

The Challenge to Current Christian Religious Education Practices

At a banquet feast, people come together to eat, which gives rise to many basic human characteristics, like kinship (who belongs to whom), language (for discussing food past, present, and future), technology (how to keep and carry food), and morality (what is just when eating together).[238] Like a banquet feast, the Church is a people who come together to participate in the drama and comedy of God's love for us in this creation. Christian religious education is about the act of following God's lead in crafting all of God's people to be the faithful, hopeful, and loving body of Christ on earth. Such education will involve teaching the Christian community to learn about kinship (who makes up the household of God and what it means to live together as God's children), language (what is our story and what does it mean to talk like a Christian), the "mechanics" of being Christians in this world (how to celebrate and share God's Gospel with one another and others), and morality (what it means to *be* Christians in this world).

In part, Christians have gone about this task by teaching the importance of cognitively knowing the content of biblical and theological truths, learned through primary individual study and group discussion, guided by a pre-set curriculum distributed by denominational offices. This way of doing Christian religious education has been and is the centerpiece of Christian religious education in the current Church. It has focused on training the intellect in enabling people to think cognitively about God. But the benefits and the price have been great. One negative result is the tendency to turn the world into an object for our investigation, analysis, and manipulation. Such a conviction neglects the world as a subject that engages people. It also depreciates the significance of symbol, myth, and rituals.[239] Those who have often been excluded from this way of learning and thinking about God, Christ, and the Holy Spirit are those with developmental, learning, physical, sensory, and emotional disabilities.

Christian religious education is not only about the task of learning God's story by the cognitive study of Scripture and theology, but also through the gestures of faith as simple as kneeling, holding hands in prayer during worship, sharing bread and a common cup together at a table set for Holy Communion, serving food in the church's soup kitchen, sewing a patch in a church's quilting workshop, and playing bells in the bell choir.[240] In practicing such gestures while actively participating in the church we learn not only *about* God's ongoing, unfolding story of love within the Christian community, we experience God in the lives of others and ourselves through relationships within the Christian community. And it is God who plays the pivotal part in shaping and nurturing our lives as invited members of the Banquet Feast. There will be more on gestures in the following chapter.

God's Banquet Feast on Earth Rearranged

This chapter has focused on Christian religious education and the person with a disability in the context of the Church. The first section of this chapter explored a more traditional, mainstreaming approach to Christian religious education with people with disabilities. This method incorporated many of the current adaptive techniques of special education and psychology with the goal of enabling the person with a disabling condition to be part of the normative, regular programs of religious education in churches.

The second approach took a more radical tack as it suggests rearranging the way we do Christian religious education in the Church, God's

Banquet on earth. Rather than fitting the person with a disabling condition into the Christian religious education program of people who are able bodied, an approach in which only those who are mildly impaired can manage, there may be an alternative that would be more truly inclusive. This involves the step of beginning to redefine an alternative description of Christian religious education that embraces and is concerned about the spiritual lives of all people, regardless of what they can and cannot do. This challenge to construct a more inclusive model of Christian religious education is spurred on by the very presence of people with disabilities who wish to share their gifts, their offering in God's Banquet Feast on earth.

Being created in the image of God, all human beings have the capacity to imagine and be creative as part of the human condition. What a person can and cannot do does not appear to be a prerequisite condition for being either imaginative or creative. What is important are the opportunities for all people to explore their God-given gifts of imagination and creativity in the context of a community of Christian believers. Yet for this imaginative interaction to occur between two or more people, human beings need to be tied into the traditions of the Christian community, not to be broken from it. Our imagination is given form and substance, is grounded in the collective stories of our past, the present experiences, and the telos of the Christian community: God's kingdom.[241]

Having set the groundwork for an alternative approach in Christian religious education with people with disabilities in the Church, this next chapter's focus will be on the act of learning the peculiar gestures of a Christian people. By learning and practicing these gestures, God's children will get a glimpse of the truly inclusive gathering, where all are invited, welcomed, and accepted. It is a gathering where all are welcomed because of who they are as God's children, not because of what they can do. It is a Banquet Feast where the doors and windows of the kingdom of God are opened to all who wish to enter and celebrate God's presence in our lives.

7

◆ ◆ ◆

Peculiar Gestures
at the Banquet Table

In much of my work with children with disabilities in the Church,
I have been taught the importance of gestures as a primary mode
of communication that, in a strange, mysterious way, connects mind,
body, spirit, and matter. From learning the importance of gestures in
my work with children with a multitude of disabilities, I began hearing
stories and watching parishioners in non-disabled congregations for
evidence of the powerful, peculiar gestures of the Church.

The first story that caught my eye and ear, had to do with George.
George was a 12-year-old boy who is labeled as having Attention Defi-
cit/Hyperactivity Disorder (AD/HD), and is also developmentally delayed. He was born and raised in a southeastern state, and was admitted
to the hospital where I once worked soon after it opened. His short,
dirty-blonde hair looks as though it were tossed on the top of his head,
and there always seem to be a trace of crumbs from his most recent
meal somewhere around his mouth. He reminds me of "Charlie
Brown's" friend "Pig Pen," for if he had the opportunity, he would
either be outside in the dirt and mud with his numerous toy trucks
and cars, or leafing through books and catalogues of pictures of truck
and car models, vividly imagining and retelling the journey of life on
the open road as a trucker. For trucks and Jesus are the love of his life.

George was forever drawing and making trucks. One of my favorite
trucks he drew around Christmas. He came into my office, quickly sat
at my desk, cleared all the papers with one large swing of his forearm,
and took out paper and pen, ready to draw a truck. But this was not
to be any truck: This was a Christian truck, which had a small cross

carefully drawn on the door and on the building located at the back end of the truck. Why did he put a church on the back of the truck? "Because we have to take God's Good News out to the people some way, so we'll put it on the back of the truck."

One night, as I was making my rounds through the hospital close to Christmas Day, George had a surprise for me. He had been hoarding empty toilet paper rolls for wheels and, with the bottom of a tissue box, a wish and a prayer, and a little glue he had scavenged, he made a truck without picture of a truck before him. He only had the pictures of trucks dancing in his mind.

As I came onto the unit, he called me over to his door and asked me to stay at the doorway to his room, close my eyes, and hold out my hands. Into my hands he put this wonderful creation, and then stood back, telling me, "Open your eyes now." With my "ahhh" of deep appreciation for the gift came a yelp of great joy from George. He was excited about his gesture of love. "Do you know what it is? Do you know what it is?" he said jumping up and down in place. "It's a truck for Jesus! For Jesus! For Jesus!" I hugged him for the beloved gift for Jesus—this "eighteen-wheeler for Jesus"—and he told me to put it on my bookshelf in my office for others to see.[242]

The second story concerns Father Bill, an Episcopal priest I met in Florida. In a sermon, he told of a transforming event in his life that took place in the First Presbyterian Church in which he was raised in Georgia. He remembered distinctly the Sunday morning worship service when he was in his early adolescence, attending worship, surrounded by all the leaders in the town. The mayor of the town, the bank president, the elders in the church, who were mostly male, did something that was extraordinary in the mind of this young boy: They stood up en masse for the affirmation of faith, using the Apostles' Creed. Young Bill heard loud and strong the voices of the men reciting the Creed, acknowledging that there was a higher authority in life than even themselves, who were already all powerful in this young boy's mind: "I believe in God, the Father Almighty, Maker of heaven and earth, and in Jesus Christ, our Lord . . ." At that moment, with the church engaged in this gesture of standing up and confessing with their lips who is Lord, Bill came to understand that God is all mighty.

Gestures: Something We Have in Common

What is of central importance in these stories is the power of gestures in the act of worshipping God. By the use of the gestures in constructing a truck and giving it to me as a gift, young George made an indelible imprint on my life and the lives of others who witnessed this great act of loving generosity. For young Bill, the gesture of the town leaders standing up together to confess what they believed regarding the author of life provided him the proof he needed and wanted for someone to direct him as to who *is* our God. Both those who are known as "disabled" and those considered "able-bodied" were given an opportunity to share their faith in God through the certain gestures of the Christian faith.

What is intriguing about gestures is that we are all dependent on them in the act of communicating with one another, no matter how old or young we are, or how limited or bright in cognitive skills, and no matter which culture we are brought up in. In regard to culture, it will be shown in this chapter that gestures are, themselves, what helps to define a culture or community like the Church and its various denominations, thus giving them the necessary borders that help identify one culture, community, or Christian denomination from another. Or as the sociologist Anthony Giddens has written, there is a double involvement of individuals and institutions: "We create society at the same time as we are created by it."[243]

As Christians, we are shaped by the gestures practiced in the context of the Church, and as we learn and practice these gestures in the church, we shape others in the Church. Theologian Steve Long understands that Christianity is not an "unchanging essence" that is able to be added into the mix of another culture. Christianity *is* a culture, "a cultivating process that produces people in a particular way." The "particular way" of Christianity is learned, communicated, and practiced by the peculiar gestures of this "community of resistance," that is called to "live the discipline" of Christ rather than adjusting it to the norms of the social order surrounding the church.[244]

The focus in this chapter will be on the importance of learning and practicing the particular gestures of the Church. This chapter on gestures is important in this book because gestures are a way of sharing and receiving the gospel among a wide range of people who reflect the natural diversity that is found among those who are invited or called to partake in God's Banquet Feast. Young and old, rich and poor, those considered "disabled" or "able-bodied" may be brought together in one place and time to worship God and participate in the educational ministry of the church, if the church is courageous enough to learn and practice the gestures of a Christian people.

What's a Gesture?

According to *Webster's Collegiate Dictionary*, a gesture is a "movement usually of the body or limbs that expresses or emphasizes an idea, sentiment or an attitude . . . something said or done by way of formality or courtesy, as a symbol or token, or for its effect on the attitudes of others."[245] The body can communicate many messages with movement, whether deliberate, such as sending a wink; inadvertent, such as blushing when embarrassed; or symbolic, as in the use of American Sign Language. The body can also communicate messages by *not* moving, such as holding one's limbs taut when someone gives you a hug.[246]

The importance of gestures in social settings has caught the imagination of many disciplines, though, by and large, there is great pioneering work that needs to be done concerning "gestures." Anthropologists, for example, understand that each community of people has certain boundary-expressing symbols, which help people to belong to a greater community. Anthropologist Anthony Cohen writes that it is in a community where one learns and continues to practice how to be in social relationships with others. It is in community that one acquires "culture," using the unique symbols and particular gestures that will equip a person to be and relate socially in the context of this community. The community is created and recreated by people through their social interaction with one another, practicing the ritualistic, gesture-filled, life of a community.[247] And anthropologist Clifford Geertz also stresses the importance of gestures in a community, and knowledge about that community. For example, when is a wink a wink, and when is a wink a twitch? For contracting one's eyelids on purpose is different than doing so reflexively. But "contracting your eyelids on purpose when there exists a public code in which so doing counts as a conspiratorial signal *is* winking. That's all there is to it: a speck of behavior, a fleck of culture, and—voila!—a gesture."[248]

To know one's culture by one's gestures is captured well in this story of the former mayor of New York City, Fiorello La Guardia. It was said that one could switch the sound off the television and still know from his gestures alone whether he was speaking English, Italian, or Yiddish.[249]

Among linguistic scholars, there is great interest regarding gestures. Walter Ong writes that a gesture is what the Statue of Liberty is engaged in doing in her historic pose in New York Harbor. Ong writes that a gesture is a far harder, more complicated form of communication, because it involves many muscular activities, often of the entire body. The beginning of the gesture, as a form of communication, comes from within a person who is engaged in an encounter with another presence; a frozen gesture, like that of the statue, has great symbolic meaning behind its placement.

For example, the Statue of Liberty is in a gesture frozen in time: There is *meaning* behind the upraised arm holding the torch of freedom. Ong writes that in "one sense it was not always thus, that the figure moved it from a lower to a higher plane and holds it there with much effort."[250]

Among speech and language professionals and special educators, there is believed to be a great deal going on in the games we play with young children, especially infants. Speech professionals Peter and Jill de Villiers write that when we play a game of peek-a-boo with a child, the child is learning true conversation: "Although the child's first words may not appear until one year-old, all during the first year he is engaged in elaborate nonverbal rituals with his caregiver that lay the groundwork for the *true* conversations."[251] The first language of children is gesture.

This is played out all the time in my house, where my one-year-old son, Parker, communicates primarily through and by gestures. To go outside, Parker will pull down his coat from a chair, take it to one of his parents, and point at the door leading outside. If he wants someone to read him a book, he will grab a book from the bookshelf, take it to the chosen reader, plop it on the reader's lap, and then physically back up to the reader, trusting that the reader will make room on his or her lap for a good read. All of this is done through gestures.

Many cartoons on television, from Mickey Mouse in "Steamboat Willie" to the "Roadrunner and Coyote" shows from my childhood days, depend upon the use of gestures and music to get across the meaning of the cartoon show, with little to no use of written or verbal language.

The importance of gesture as language is explored by neuropsychiatrist Oliver Sacks in his book concerning the deaf culture in America, *Seeing Voices.* Sacks writes that there has been a great debate since the

19th century as to what came first, physical gestures or spoken words, as a form of language. Sign language, used by many in the hearing-impaired community, originated as a formalized pattern of gestures, which is highly iconic. In other words, each gesture in American Sign Language, for example, *means* something. Sign language gestures are so powerful a portrayal of speech that they have no analogue in or cannot be translated into the language of speech.[252] The frustration with this issue is that the spoken word is also a gesture, as the facial muscles must move in various ways in order that the air and noise that we exhale and inhale may flow. And, as written earlier, if facial muscles like grimaces or smiles are gestures, is it not possible to consider that the words we speak are also a form of gesture?

In the Bible, there are plenty of stories where the biblical characters are engaged in the act of practicing gestures in order to make their point, or God's point, clear for all to see and experience. For example, one of the most dramatic stories in the Hebrew Bible concerns Abraham and Isaac. Abraham, doing what God had shown him, built an altar and laid wood, then bound his son Isaac and placed him on the altar. "Then Abraham reached out his hand and took the knife to kill his son" (Genesis 22:10). God also performed many miracles through Moses and Aaron, using bodily gestures to bring forth the intended results. For example, there is the first plague, where the water is turned to blood, by Moses taking his staff and stretching out his hand over the waters of Egypt (Ex. 7:19); and the second plague, when he stretched his hand out with the staff in it over the river, the canals, and the pools and made frogs come up on the land of Egypt (Ex. 8:7). Finally, Moses stretched out his hand over the sea and "the Lord drove the sea back by a strong east wind all night, and turned the sea into dry land; and the waters were divided" (Ex. 14:21).

In the New Testament, we see Jesus performing many acts of faith through and by the use of gestures. For example, there is Peter, walking on the water during a storm, coming toward Jesus, when he noticed the strong wind and became frightened, crying "Lord, save me!" We read that Jesus immediately reached out his hand and caught him, saying "You of little faith, why did you doubt?" (Matthew 14:28–33). Or Jesus healed people not by words only, but often by the gesture of touch, as when Jesus healed two blind men. After crying, "Have mercy upon us, Lord, Son of David!" Jesus stood still and called them, saying "What do you want me to do for you?" They said to him, "Lord, let our eyes be opened." And we read that Jesus, who was moved with compassion, touched their eyes, a gesture. Immediately, we read, they regained their sight and followed him (Matthew 20:29–34).

One of the most powerful, gestureful stories in the Gospel accounts of Jesus' ministry, concerns the institution of the Lord's Supper. We read *what* Jesus did—he took a loaf of bread, and "when he had given thanks, he broke it and gave it to them [the disciples], saying, 'This is my body, which is given for you. Do this in remembrance of me'" (Luke 22:19). Jesus did the same with the cup, saying that "the cup poured out for you is the new covenant in my blood" (Luke 22:20). Jesus even indicated that there was one who was going to betray him, by acknowledging the gesture of his hand being on the table where they had all eaten (Luke 22:21). To this day, in the Church universal, this meal is still being celebrated, copying the gestures we believe Jesus may have used, accompanied by the words of institution of this sacrament, with breaking of the bread, and pouring wine into a cup.

The Apostle Paul understood that the Church, this body of Christ on earth, was going to need to be exercised in order that we Christians would remember exactly whose we are. For example, one of the phrases recited by the early Church at a baptism was from Romans 13:14: "Put on the Lord Jesus Christ." By saying this, as the theologian Karl Barth wrote, what is happening at Baptism is that Christ is put on us in the context of the Church.[253] This assumes there is an action, a bodily gesture, in which Christ is put on us, and we grow into Christ. In Philippians 4:9, Paul tells the people, "Keep on doing the things that you have learned and received and heard and seen in me, and the God of peace will be with you." The promise here is on the doing, as a way of having a greater understanding of the gift of grace and faith we have been given by God in Christ. Throughout his letters, Paul exhorts Christ's people to keep on doing the things of Christ, because we believe that Christ is present in these acts. As we believe, practice, and act courageously on the good news of the Gospel, the God of peace will be with us as we do these things.

The Church continues to practice the gestures of faith that it was told to practice by the Apostle Paul throughout history. The sacraments of the Church are themselves gesture-filled exercises of the body of Christ that makes followers of Christ more certain of the trusting nature of God's Word. The Reformed theologian John Calvin wrote that because we are flesh, we have a dull capacity, and need to be led by the hand "as tutors lead children." Quoting St. Augustine, Calvin cites that the sacraments, these bodily gestures are a "visible word" for the "reason that it represents God's promises as painted in a picture and sets them before our sight, portrayed graphically and in the manner of images."[254] The sacraments are the mirrors in which we may contemplate the riches of God's grace, "which he lavishes upon us. For by them he manifests himself to us as far as our dullness is given to perceive, and attests his good will and love toward us more expressly than by word."[255]

Today, the Church is still dependent on the gestures of the Christian faith for correcting our lives from the natural crookedness of our walk as we journey toward the kingdom of God. Theologian Stanley Hauerwas writes that in the sacraments of Baptism and Eucharist, we are initiated and reconstituted into Jesus' life, death, and resurrection. Hauerwas writes that these are the essential gestures of the Christian life, and that we cannot be the church of Christ without them. The liturgy of the church becomes more than simply another ritual in the habitual life we live: Liturgy is social action that takes our contorted, skewed perception of the Christian life and realigns us so that we may live rightly the story of God.[256]

Gestures are important to our human life in general and to the Christian culture in particular. The method by which we communicate to others our thoughts, feelings, and faith is by bodily gestures, and most of the ideas and perceptions that shape and influence our lives are these very same gestures exercised by others we are in relationship with in our busy lives. What is fascinating in focusing on these gestures is the realization that the exercise of gestures is quite universal among human beings of all ages, in all communal contexts, and most of the time regardless of one's abilities or limitations. Young George, who is considered "disabled," revealed to all around him in his gesture of gift giving, his knowledge of Jesus' love, and his own love for Jesus. Able-bodied Bill was transformed by the simple practice of the gesture of standing up during the congregational confession of faith using the Apostles' Creed. In this next section, the focus will be on the sacraments and educational practices of congregations and parishes as they learn and practice the gestures of faith that are particular and peculiar to Christian people.

Practicing Gestures of a Christian People

As we explore various gestures that may be practiced in the context of the Church, it is important to note that there will be some resistance to this focus because many in the Church have focused solely on the written and verbal methods of communication. They have not been schooled to understand and appreciate the complexity of practicing Christian gestures, such as knowing when it is appropriate to extend the hand of friendship in the church as well as when to withhold it; the value of kneeling in prayer; the value of quietly embracing someone who is struck by grief and needs only a hand to hold or a hug from someone courageous enough to stand in the face of such pain; or even the value of the rhythm of the liturgy used to guide us in worship of God.

The peculiar skills of showing honor, living in harmony, admonishing one another, giving holy kisses, waiting for people, being servants to one another, bearing one another's burdens, being at peace and sharing it with someone else in confession, praying and having fellowship with those who are not like us are all gestures that need to be learned. As Hauerwas writes, we must be taught the gestures that help position our bodies and our souls to be able to hear rightly and retell God's Story. Even learning how to pray depends on one's need to learn how to pray, learning how to bend the body: "Learning the gesture and posture of prayer is inseparable from *learning* to pray. Indeed, the gestures are prayers.[257]

These gestures are best learned and practiced in the context of a community of believers. For by our gestures we are engaged with one another, and with the One, who all help to create and form the community that gives our lives meaning. We could learn and practice these gestures like the !Kung do in Africa, where there is *constant* interaction between adult and child, adult and adolescents, and adolescent and child. They all play and dance together, sit together, participate in minor hunting together, join in storytelling together. There are also times when children are party to rituals controlled by adults, like the first haircutting or the boy's first killing of a buck. Writes psychologist Jerome Bruner: "Children . . . are constantly playing imitatively with the rituals, implements, tools, and weapons of the adult world."[258] Nobody teaches in the prepared sense of the word. There is nothing like school, nothing like lessons; in fact, there is very little "telling" among the !Kung. Instead of telling children *out* of context, the !Kung prefer to *show* the children *in* context.[259]

If the Church chooses to focus intentionally on "putting on the Lord Jesus Christ," as the Apostle Paul put it, then children and adults will need to be engaged in learning the gestures of the Christian faith by practicing the gestures in the company of others who either need to learn them or continue to practice them. With the purpose of learning and practicing the gestures of the Church among those considered "disabled" or "able-bodied," then here are some suggestions for the congregation or parish:

Practice and Celebrate the Rubrics of the Church in the Company of Members of the Body of Christ

By rubrics, I mean the gestures that are part of the established rules, traditions, rituals, or customs of the church that are part of the liturgy of the church in worship.

In worship, it is important to remember that not everyone can read the bulletin, decipher the symbols on the page, nor balance two or more books during worship, especially while trying to participate in the liturgy. If liturgy is truly "the work of the people" in worshipping God, then its gestures will need to be learned and practiced by the people of God over and over again as people develop a habit in practicing it.

In established worship services, people depend on the liturgy following certain physical habits: People stand or sit for the "Call of Worship"; parishioners reach out and shake hands, hug, or even kiss someone on the cheek when "Passing the Peace of Christ." In some Christian traditions, people kneel and bow during a prayer, some making a slight bow when the cross of Christ passes before them. People often stand when confessing what they believe in the Apostles' Creed, waiting for the celebrant or minister to tell them when to sit. Finally, people wait for the minister or priest to bless them before they leave to go out into the world.

Celebrate the Sacraments of the Church

For most Protestant and Reformed churches, the two sacraments are Baptism and Eucharist, which are shared with other Christian traditions as well. In the following chapter, there is a discussion about the Eucharist as our common meal, where we all confess our sinful, broken, crippled condition before God in Christ.

Baptism is also important in the life of the Church. In 1982, the World Council of Churches developed the manual, *Baptism, Eucharist and Ministry*.[260] The manual maintains that Baptism has two purposes:

first, on a personal level, it is seen as a sign of new life through Christ, who went down to the Jordan River and was baptized. Once baptized, the person will be ultimately one with Christ as the individual is nurtured and guided by the Holy Spirit. Second, one is baptized into the body of Christ, in which the congregation acknowledges we are members of one another. We are engrafted in the true vine. Thus, Baptism is a sign and seal of our common discipleship with others. When people with disabilities are baptized, they are recognized not only as a member of a particular church, but the church itself reaffirms its faith in God, and God's gift of grace, pledging itself to provide an environment of witness and service to the life of the newly baptized members.

Baptism is important, first of all, as a gesture-centered action of the church, where water is the symbol of the Jordan River for the "washing away of sins," and the minister than sprinkling or immersing the person with a disability in the water. Even the person who has profound limitations will react to the touch of water on his or her body, bringing forth a response, from a smile or a scream of delight, to a cry or shriek of fear. The fact that there is a response is important. For this simple gesture has made an impression on the life of the person with a disability, and on the minds and hearts of the congregation.

This sacramental gesture of baptism is important for the family of the person with a disability and the congregation, as the congregation witnesses the truth that this child or person with a disability is, first and foremost, a child of God, and part of the ongoing narrative of the Christian faith. The family and congregation pledge to provide an environment of witness and service for the life of the person with a disability.[261]

Be Careful! You Are Acting Out the Gospel Stories

When reading the scriptures in church, ministers and lay readers alike need to be aware that people are watching the gestures used for reading the stories as well as listening to and for the Word of God. People are watching body posture, hand gestures, listening to the tone of voice, looking for grimaces and smiles on the face, as much as they are listening to the words that are being read. People are always tuning into the gestures or speech-acts of the preacher and lay reader.

For an example of the intricacy of communication, consider the story, "The President's Speech," from Oliver Sacks's book, *The Man Who Mistook His Wife for a Hat*. In watching a speech by former President Reagan, a ward of people with global aphasia were laughing hysterically. Global aphasia renders people incapable of understanding words, listening instead to the tone of voice, intonation, emphasis on inflection, "as well as all visual cues (one's expressions, one's gestures, one's entire, largely unconscious, personal repertoire and posture)."[262] In other words, the power of understanding to these people is understanding, without words, what is authentic or unauthentic. "Thus it was the grimaces, the histrionisms, the false gestures and, above all, the false tones and cadences of the voice, which rang false for these wordless but immensely sensitive patients. It was to these [for them] most glaring, even grotesque, incongruities and improprieties that my aphasic patients responded, undeceived and undeceivable by words. This is why they laughed at the President's speech."[263]

It may help to role play or act out the Scripture rather than always reading it from the pulpit. The use of skits, whether in worship or in other activities at church, may be helpful so that more people may understand and receive the story of God as recorded in the Bible.

The Church and All the Gestureful Acts of Faith

Making and baking bread for Holy Communion or Eucharist; taking someone along to make a visit to the hospital, retirement village, or nursing home; visiting a residential center for children and adolescents with disabilities; engaging in the local Habitat for Humanity project, the community's soup kitchen or homeless shelter, or visiting an AIDS hospice are all gestures of the Christian Church. These are all ways that the Banquet Feast of God's love extends beyond the physical walls of the church building, and is found in some of the most unlikely places in the world. In the Gospel of Matthew, in the portion called "The Commissioning of the Disciples," Jesus is instructing the disciples to continue to practice the gestures that would mark his followers for life: to *make* disciples of all nations, *baptizing* them . . . and teaching them to *obey* everything that Jesus commanded. To make, to baptize, to obey are not actions done to get to the kingdom of God only, but are done because Jesus has already saved us, and reminds us that as we practice these gestures, we do not do them alone: "And remember, I am with you always, to the end of the age" (Matthew 28:20).

Gestures as Christian Manners at the Banquet Table

In a recent column on manners and etiquette, "Miss Manners" wrote that a world that is "uncontaminated by etiquette" is a world in trouble:

We find out every day, with the shoves, shouts and fingers offered by those who feel free to talk and behave as their uninhibited impulses suggest.

We observe it when trying to follow such basic social practices as offering hospitality and giving presents, only to find that the responsive half—answering invitations, showing up when promised, offering thanks, reciprocating—is not, after all, the natural reaction to generosity.

What seems to be natural is a ferocious selfishness that, now unbridled, is turning births, weddings and even deaths into fundraisers, and religious holidays into occasions for self-pity.

Living without rules of etiquette, or manners, is seen, in this social columnist's mind as a recipe for disaster. For "finally abandoning the idea that all we need for harmonious living is to bring out truly unsocialized human nature, [we will] find [ourselves] with three weapons: counter-rudeness, violence and [for the fastidious and long-pocketed] lawsuits." In looking at violence, she writes that "while violence often silences the original offender forever, it, too, has done little for the quality of life."[264]

Etiquette, or the gestureful manners we learn in the context of society, is similar to the gesture we learn in the context of the church, God's Banquet Feast on earth. One could say that learning and practicing the Christian gestures of the church are the "table manners" and "etiquette" necessary for learning how best to enjoy the sumptuous feast of God's grace and love at the Banquet Table. For like society, if the church members were free to act on their feelings, saying what they really meant, doing what they really want to do, then we would no longer need to pray in the Lord's Prayer to be led away from temptation of evil, for we have raised temptation as a god to be worshipped. Instead, we need to understand that we are a people, regardless of our abilities or limitations, who confess our inherent weakness and are in need of a God who alone can lead us away from evil, and who, when we are led into the ways of evil, can alone forgive us for "our trespasses."

The practice of Christian gestures has power not because of our actions solely, but because we learn and practice these gestures because Jesus has been raised from the dead, and we continue to exercise these gestures, that have tremendous power, because of our courage in the power of the Gospel to transform our communal lives. It was the practice of the gestures in cutting out, pasting, and giving a gift that shaped both George's and my perception of the limitless imagination of God, instilled in the simple act of a child labeled "disabled." It was the repetitive practice of the gesture of standing up together, and reciting in unison what they confess is their faith, that transformed young Bill's perception of God from a "given god" to the Almighty, "Maker of heaven and earth." These gestures, based on God's story, have shaped and are shaping all of our lives into the ways of Truth and love, which is communicated and reinforced in powerful ways in the eucharistic meal as discussed in the closing chapter.

8

◆ ◆ ◆

Celebrating with the Expected Guests: Toward an Inclusive Congregational Life

In the first chapter of this book, I began with stories of pain and struggle, where people with disabilities and their families were the uninvited and unwelcomed guests to God's Banquet Feast on earth, left outside of the life of their respective Christian communities. However, that is not the end of the story, nor any way to end a book.

This final chapter ends on many notes of hope, anticipating changes in God's Banquet on earth among congregations who, willingly and consciously, invite and include those with disabilities into the daily activities of congregational life. In the following stories, there is a spirit of companionship among people, both those with disabilities and those who are non disabled. "Companion" literally means "a person with whom we share bread."[265] Breaking bread and sharing it with friends actually means friendship itself, within a spirit of trust, pleasure, and gratitude in the act of sharing.[266] In the "breaking of the bread" during Holy Communion, we recognize not only that we are sharing the bread of life among friends, but proclaiming a companionship with Jesus Christ, who is the actual, living bond that unites us.

In this spirit of companionship, I begin with a story of Holy Communion, a meal in which we all come as we are, longing to be with Jesus.

Partaking in the Lord's Supper As New Friends in Christ

The celebration of the Lord's Supper has been a place where, more than once, new lessons were learned by members of Christ's community. One moving account of Holy Communion happened in one small Presbyterian church in Missouri right after Easter. A small group of Christians had gathered together on Maundy Thursday, and the young pastor told me the story of the transformational experience that occurred during the sacrament of Holy Communion with a young boy with Down's syndrome. Unlike most Sunday worship services, on this day there was only a small group of Christians gathered together and so they came around the table in the front of the sanctuary that is used for the Lord's Supper. Suddenly, it struck the pastor that not only was she coming to seek forgiveness and healing in her life, but so was this young boy who was mentally retarded. She realized for the first time that what she shared with this young boy she had rarely communicated with is a common dependence on God's gift of grace, now discovered in the process of justification and sanctification through the actions taken in the ritual of the Lord's Supper. No longer were these abstract, theological concepts: They were now concrete needs.

The Importance of Being a Crucifer

This story is about 15-year-old Michelle. The picture in my mind when I think of Michelle is of a young woman wearing a white alb, with a small cross pendant hanging around her neck, just like the other young people who are participants in the rituals of this small Episcopal church in Florida. Underneath the alb, she is wearing her dirty white tennis shoes, just like the other young people do. And she is responsible, at least once a month, for being the crucifer in worship, carrying the cross of Christ down the aisle during worship, just like the other young people do. What is *not* like the other young people is that Michelle has Down's syndrome. Yet, within this small parish, that fact of life doesn't seem to influence or persuade the priest or anyone else in the congregation that she shouldn't be an active part of leading worship like her peers do. She is an active part of congregational life, attending worship even when she doesn't have a leading part in the ritual, just like any other young person in the church.

Discovering a Place in the Body of Christ

This story concerns George, a young man who is 19 years old, living with his mother, and attending a small, charismatic church in Florida. George is a Christian who believes that the Lord "made me for a purpose." This powerful statement of faith is made even more powerful when one realizes that George has some autistic behavior, which means that he is somewhat restricted in his ability to communicate with others. Like other children with autistic-like behaviors, George exhibits self-stimulating behavior, such as repeatedly saying "record play," while tapping his front two teeth and rocking in place.

However, unbeknownst to George's mother, her parents, and the church they attend, George has been watching and listening to most everything in life that has been occurring around and to him for the past 19 years. We know that George has been aware and learning from his experiences in life because of his ability to use facilitated communication. This controversial new method is similar to the hunt-and-peck method of typing on an old manual typewriter. What is different is that the typing is done on a hand-held portable computer with a little ticker tape that produces the typed message. Some health-service providers see it as a pen—a quill of sorts. Simply by someone else holding the hand, elbow, or shoulder, those with autism are able to communicate what they think, feel, and believe.

With the knowledge that George is able to understand many things about this world and, in a limited way, communicate with others, he has been welcomed into the church in new ways. He is now invited to be with the other men of the church in their Bible studies, and not with the preschool children, though he still enjoys playing with them as well. He is able to join in prayer services and worship services of praise and draw very little attention, because people know that he is able to understand much of what is happening around him. And what is his place in the body of Christ? George understands that he is "the ear," because he has spent much of his life listening to everyone and, up to this point, has had no opportunity to talk with or to others.

The Fine Art of Celebrating

Kyle, a member of the l'Arche community in London, is an important part of any celebration within l'Arche or the church he attends.

One of the Roman Catholic priests connected with l'Arche told me the story of his installation service in a London suburb. At the beginning of this formal and high church service, things were subdued and sedate . . . until ten minutes into the service when the l'Arche community suddenly burst into the sanctuary and hurried down the aisle to the front, greeting people with hugs and kisses, shaking hands, and bringing "the joy of the Lord to worship." Leading the l'Arche procession was Kyle, a man with mental retardation, who is truly willing and able to celebrate life; in truth, this is his gift to the l'Arche community and the Church.

I witnessed his keen sense of celebration in a Baptism in the Anglican church that some in the l'Arche community attend. All was quiet as the priest held a baby, with the parents and extended family gathered around the baptismal font. Soon, right in the midst of things, there was Kyle, leaning in and watching carefully all that was happening. As the priest finished saying the words of the ritual of Baptism, Kyle uttered a sound that seemed to be a "Waaaay!," clapping his hands and smiling with a broad smile. And with that, he was joined by others in the parish gathered around the family and the priest, announcing and celebrating the new member in the body of Christ.

Let the Children Come

This story is of a good struggle that is occurring in a suburban United Methodist church in Wilmington, Delaware. The pastor's wife first told me of the struggle that was arising within the church school program over the inclusion of children with disabling conditions in the Christian religious education program. On the one side of the struggle were the parents of the children with disabilities and the Sunday School teachers who were making their case for the presence of these children in the Sunday School class. On the other side were the parents of the children who were not disabled. What has made an impression on all concerned is the response of the children without disabilities to the presence of children with disabilities: a caring response. In the church playground, the children were all playing together and helping one another, living out Jesus' commandment to "love your neighbor as yourself."

In this church, there is a young boy who is eight years old and is severely mentally retarded. One of the teachers told the story of what happened at Vacation Bible School this past summer, when, in the

middle of worship, this young boy came up and wanted to just hold
the Bible: he wanted to be included in worship, doing something, and
the worship leader welcomed his help. There are other children that
are present in the congregation, like a 10-year-old girl with Down's
syndrome who loves to play with the other children in the playground.
There are numerous children with learning problems and learning disabilities, and others with Attention Deficit/Hyperactivity Disorder who
attend the church, and whose parents expect these children to be in
the Sunday School program. Currently, there are 15 to 18 children in
many of the classes, with one or two teachers. The strategy at this
time is to include the parents of these children to work on a one-on-
one (1:1) or one-teacher-to-two-children (1:2) basis, with the goal of
including these children rather than segregating them from their peers.
Why? The teachers and the children understand that this is an opportunity to receive and welcome the God-given gifts of these young members who are disabled. They are practicing Holy gestures.

Signs of God's Banquet Feast on Earth

Something *is* happening in many congregations and parishes that
are struggling to learn how to extend the invitation of friendship, and,
in so doing, welcoming and accepting those with disabilities in the life
of largely non-disabled congregations, as brothers and sisters in Christ.
In the small Presbyterian church, the presence of the young boy with
Down's syndrome enabled even the well-educated pastor to come to a
new understanding of the significance of the Lord's Supper.

In the Episcopal parish, the lack of fanfare around the presence of
Michelle revealed that it *is* possible for people with disabilities to just
be a member of a church, with no special programs or "best buddies"
systems in place.

George, the young man with autistic behavior, is being given a place
among the other young men in the church as the church is willing to
struggle to reenvision George not as a two-year-old toddler but as a
19-year-old young man.

Kyle redefines the meaning of worship in general, and Baptism in
particular, for an entire Anglican community in London.

Finally, there is the story of the Methodist church shifting its approach in Christian religious education to include children with disabilities in the traditional Sunday School program; they are opting to be

"like Jesus" in even welcoming the children with disabilities into the Sunday School activities.

One of the important and powerful lessons learned from these encouraging stories is that the Christian community does not have to come up with yet one more ritual or traditional meal for welcoming and embracing the presence of people with disabilities. The Church already *has* in its traditions a ritualistic meal that has been celebrated throughout the ages, in all cultures: Holy Communion or Eucharist. In the celebration of this Holy meal, more hearts and minds have been opened among those participating as to the essential place and necessary presence of people with disabilities in our congregations and parishes. As Stanley Hauerwas wrote about people with mental retardation: "If the World [of God] is preached and the sacraments served without the presence of the mentally handicapped then it may be we are less than the body of Christ."[267]

Gathering Around
the Common Table of the Lord

In the translator's notes in the front of Michel Jeanneret's book, *A Feast of Words*, there is the following translation of the word "Banquet":

> In French it carries an allusion to Plato, whose *Symposium* is translated as Le Banquet: "le banquet eucharistique" is the equivalent of "the Eucharistic Feast" in devotional English—"feast," with its overtones of "love-feast" and "feasting with friends," might be a closer English alternative.[268]

In the Christian community, there is a sacramental ritual that calls on and challenges the collective imagination of a congregation and parish: Christ's community is called to imagine a feast on earth in which we believe that Christ's Spirit is with us in the breaking of bread and drinking of wine in the name of Jesus. This is a love-feast of sorts that is extended to all baptized members from all directions on the earth: north and south, east and west. This sacrament is celebrated in both the Roman Catholic and Protestant church and is known by various names, like Eucharist, the Lord's Supper, or Holy Communion. Around the Lord's Supper, all believers come to eat a meal that involves not only our basic human need for food, but for each other and, most importantly, for God. We all need God's presence to fill the emptiness and heal the wounds of our broken lives.

In one of the l'Arche communities in France, the community members work hard with those with mental retardation to live out a theology of the Eucharist. The ability to comprehend and participate in the Eucharistic meal is not taken lightly in l'Arche. I remember sitting in on a confirmation lesson with three other people who were severely or profoundly mentally retarded and multiply disabled. Surrounding the participants were large crosses and icons of Jesus' and the Virgin Mary's face, all in view of the people with disabilities seated in large beanbag chairs on the floor. Candles were brightly burning and the room was filled with the smells of incense intermingled with the odor of freshly cut flowers. There was a cup of wine and pieces of freshly baked bread near the assistants, who would hold these elements up to the noses and eyes of the people with disabilities. They physically placed the elements in the hands of the people with disabilities as well, and then searched their faces to see if there was any reaction to this stimulus, like a wink of an eye, a slight facial grimace, or a shaking of a body part in recognition of these elements. What was amazing was that there usually was some physical response, though small, by the person with a disability, which the assistants rejoiced over.

What this story from l'Arche, as well as the story of the Presbyterian congregation reveals is that, on the one hand, there is the hopeful sign of people with disabling conditions like mental retardation not only participating in the Eucharistic celebration, but comprehending what is happening. On the other hand, what is also being affirmed is the acknowledgement of the Presbyterian pastor: she needed the presence of the person with a disabling condition to remind her that both of them, because of their mortal condition, are in need of the love of God that, alone, can bring the sweet taste of forgiveness in the mouth of the Christian. Given the title and overriding metaphor of this book, God's Banquet Feast, we have a wonderful ongoing example in the Lord's Supper that continually reminds all who participate in this meal of their dependent relationship with God in Christ. After all the exercises and activities have been tried from this book, it appears that congregations and parishes already have a ritual that will continually bring home the point to all Christians that this is a reconciling meal, where the one disabled and the able-bodied together may find reconciliation and the joy that has eluded them in other endeavors in this world. Their joy is found in the living presence of Christ's Spirit in their midst around this common meal.

The source of this Eucharistic meal is found in the synoptic Gospels (Matthew, Mark, and Luke), and the meal has gone by various names in these texts, like "the Last Supper," and "the meal in the Upper Room."[269] One account of the initial meal recorded it as being more of a meal of friendship than a Passover seder meal; an informal gathering of friends who came together for special reasons of commitment and charity. The breaking of the bread, pouring of the wine, and the blessings were not that unusual, but quite natural.[270]

What was *not* natural were the words that Jesus used to identify that the bread was his body, and the wine was his blood, which presented the disciples, and followers throughout the ages, with a completely radical way of understanding life. The day after this meal, Jesus himself became a sacrifice for all of creation, a sacrifice that is done but not over. In this sacrifice was born the incarnational relationship of humankind with God, which God initiated through the life, death, and resurrection of Jesus Christ.[271]

By coming around the table and joining in the eating and drinking of these elements, Christians join the communion of saints in celebrating and remembering proof of God's ongoing love for humankind. The words embodied a new covenant between God and humankind as the divine effort to call humanity to a participation in a cosmic commonweal.[272] The theologian Geoffrey Wainwright considers the Eucharist an experience where God has given of God's self, as both gift and giver: "God enters into the very marrow of our being yet remains inexhaustible."[273]

However, the meal is not only food for today, but revels in an anticipation of what is to come. Wainwright reminds us that the Eucharist is an anticipatory concretion of a heavenly feast with God: "Our expectation is increased precisely because we already have the promise, the pledge, the earnest, the taste. We have started to enjoy God."[274] Even though the appearance of God's Spirit in our lives may appear spotty and occasional, there are miraculous moments when the Kingdom of God, the unexpected yet anticipated messianic banquet, becomes present.

The scholar Margaret Visser writes that the eucharistic celebration is a dinner "at which table manners are entirely necessary; for nothing like it . . . can begin to be imagined unless the people participating in it commit themselves, both now and in future, to behaving."[275] As we behave in the repeated eucharistic celebration, people's very lives continue to be shaped and nurtured as members of Christ's community. Wainwright writes that the Eucharist is important in what it makes of us, for what happens in this meal is that the future of God's kingdom takes precedence in our lives; we now know the course for the future, and that future is God and God's kingdom.[276]

For those people with disabilities, this meal is as important as it is for the person who is non-disabled. What is exciting about this eucharistic celebration is that it concretizes for all involved what the community of Christ *should* look, feel, and be like. It gives all involved a taste of forgiveness for the wrongs committed against one another, when people were aware of what they had done and not done against their neighbor. There emerges a reconciling love that binds all people's hearts together as one in God's Spirit. This love fills all involved in the journey towards wholeness and spiritual well-being.[277]

Will the person who is severely mentally retarded or multiply disabled comprehend what is happening? Frederick Buechner writes that when it comes to the act of forgiving and the transforming love of God, "one wonders if the 6-week-old screecher knows all that much less than the Archbishop of Canterbury."[278] What happens at the eucharistic meal remains a mystery, yet we carry on with this ritual in Christian faith, believing and anticipating that all of us will be welcomed at the messianic banquet "which is the glorious liberty of God's children in his kingdom."[279]

Extending an Invitation to Others Outside the Church

In the parable of the Banquet Feast, Jesus recounts that when the slave has come back and told the Host that what was ordered has been done, and there is still room, "then the master said to the slave, 'Go out into the road and lanes, and compel people to come in, so that my house may be filled'" (Luke 14:23). The slave was to go out once again and *compel* people to come.[280]

Taking our cue from this direct hint from this parable, Christians are called to compel those within our congregations and parishes who are disabled but who no longer come to our churches to come back.

This is the call to evangelism, including those with disabilities, for there is a place for all people at God's Banquet Feast on earth, an alternative community where we have the time to care for and be cared for by one another.

This passage is very important in regard to this issue of evangelism. As the body of Christ on earth, we are the servant who is ordered by the Host to compel people to come, especially those with disabilities, who is often the stranger in the crowd. To put it another way, members of the Church can't say "You can't worship" to people with disabling conditions.[281] The Church is composed of people whose sacred narrative tells them that "the stranger that sojourns with you shall be unto you as the homeborn among you" (Leviticus). This message is repeated by Jesus who told his followers that when they took care of those who were sick, neglected, and alone, that "just as you did it to one of the least of these who are members of my family, you did it to me" (Matt. 25:40).

Reaching out and being Christ's community with people with disabilities is an important issue now, given the way that many in the world perceive people with any kind of disabling condition. In this final section, there will be a review of disturbing trends in the surrounding society that has direct implications for people with disabilities. Standing against the tide of social trends is the Church, which becomes a sanctuary, truly a safe haven for people with disabilities. In order to let others know of the concern that the Church has for brothers and sisters with disabilities, an invitation is extended to the disability community, in hopes of welcoming and accepting all who are invited to God's Banquet.

A World View of People with Disabilities

The crucial task facing the Church is to go out into the world and reach out to those people with disabilities, their respective families, and the professional health service providers who are called to care for people with disabling conditions. And the world in general is in need of hearing and seeing the Christian community struggle with the inclusion of people with disabilities and come up with some imaginative ways of welcoming and accepting them. For society lacks the basis for knowing how to care for those with disabilities as there are few examples to become a catalyst for stretching society's imagination.[282]

For example, sometimes it appears that the only calling many people with mental retardation can respond to in terms of using their gifts and abilities is by finding work at a fast-food establishment, like McDonald's and Burger King. There are still too many vocational, sheltered workshops and not enough art studios, music centers, and theaters for people with disabilities. This is all because society has often dictated that the worth of all people is discovered in what they can *do* in society; our value and identity, even among those with disabilities, is defined by the work or job that we have and not in who we *are* in the community. The larger society does not see nor understand what it means to *be in* communion with one another as we are made to be together.[283]

Furthermore, society seems to be less and less tolerant of people who are different. Society seems to no longer be able to accept differences, with the realm of abnormal encroaching on and defining that which was once considered normal, an individual choice, a habit, eccentricity, or lifestyle issue. As was mentioned earlier in the book, the social science of classification and labeling of different conditions appears to be spreading out of control, supported by many health-service professionals in fields like psychiatry and psychology. In a world that feels that its health-care resources are stretched to their maximum efficiency, there is more and more talk of consciously rationing health care, where some will get the care they need and others won't due to their condition. The fear among many in the disability community is that they will be among those who are not covered in universal health insurance programs, and therefore will not receive the care they need due to their previous condition.

In the field of medicine, the human genome project is either a potential help or threat to people with mental retardation, because it may encourage the presumption "that people should regulate their sexual and marital behavior to avoid having handicapped children":

> What will our society say to those who decide to challenge the presuppositions that we ought to avoid having mentally handicapped children? It is possible to envision that society may well put legal and financial penalties on people who decide to have children that are less than "normal."[284]

There is great fear among many who work with people with disabilities that social Darwinistic thought is thriving in our society, and that the only children who should be allowed to be born and not aborted, and allowed to live and not die, are those who fit the social demands of being healthy . . . birth becomes the arena in which only the fittest and healthiest survive. It is no wonder, then, that many people with disabling conditions feel less than human, overwhelmed by the negative remarks they carry as a yoke of oppression placed upon them by a society that devalues their very existence.

The Radical Stance of the Church

In the midst of this bleak, dark picture the candlelight of God's Banquet Feast in the Church pierces through the murkiness of society. What is striking about the Church in the midst of this social gloom is the very company who are called and come together around God's banquet feast of love.

The invitations to the feast in the parable, and the Banquet Feast of the Church today, displays a random and open commensalism that is most startling to the people who still hear the biblical story of the Banquet Feast. Just as the focus of this parable was as an egalitarian challenge to society's hierarchy and social rituals that leave out those who are different from you and me, so the Banquet Feast of God's love challenges the normative order of society.

The biblical scholar John Dominic Crossan writes that Jesus was rightly charged by many in the surrounding Jewish society of not making appropriate distinctions and discriminations among the people that he was seen with. Jesus was seen talking and eating with the outcasts of society: the tax collector, the prostitute, the people who were sick, disabled, and in poverty, and even with the Sadducees and Pharisees. It was said that Jesus had no honor, no shame.[285] The Church, whose very model is the life of Jesus, includes people with disabilities, welcoming others with no distinction or discrimination. In doing so, it becomes a living symbol of Christ in the world, for like Jesus, the Church has little honor in the eyes of many in the world.

However, this harsh reaction by society is good news for the Church, for this is exactly what Jesus wanted to get across to those who follow him regarding the nature of God's kingdom: in God's Kingdom there will be no rich and poor; no rank or status will exist among people; there will be no distinction and hierarchy between female and male, poor and rich, Gentile and Jew. God's Kingdom is one of love among all believers in the presence of Divine love.[286]

As Jesus' stories challenged the believers in an earlier age, this story which guides the actions of the Christian community continues to challenge the status quo and hierarchies today, even within the Church. And the congregation or parish that struggles and perseveres, that celebrates and rejoices with others in the act of inviting and welcoming people with disabilities, especially those who are severely or multiply disabled and poor, will appear "strange" in the eyes of the world, yet more like Jesus in God's perception.

In being more like Jesus, the Church has an opportunity to extend an invitation to people with disabilities in the world:

To extend an invitation for a new way of understanding the human condition: Rather than rejecting or pitying those with a disabling condition and their families, the Church opens its arms and is wildly enthusiastic in celebrating their presence in our midst, for they come not as objects of charity, but as companions at a meal.

The Church believes that all people are created in the image of God. Because each person is created in the image of God, one's very being is precious as all life is God's gift. In the Christian community each person is precious. For it is in the Christian community that we each discover and love the secret of what is unique in ourselves as a creation of God's love. [287]

As was mentioned earlier in the book, the gift that people with disabling conditions bring with them in their mere presence at the meal is a call to love and be loved by others; to serve and be served by others; to listen and be listened to by others; to liberate and be liberated by others in Christ. Thus, the Church does not envision the person with a disability as a heavy burden or a draining weakness: in the context of the Church the person with a disability is a gift, for he or she often calls others to *be* the body of Christ, the Banquet Feast incarnate. Unlike the surrounding society, where those with disabilities are considered a drag on limited resources of health care, the Church celebrates the joy of another member around the Banquet Feast.

To extend an invitation to a new way of living with one another: The Christian community thrives on diversity, on weakness, on including the stranger. The Christian community needs this sense of insecurity and doubt, of fear and wonder, for this is the way of God. The problem for many congregations is that they are weakest when they exclude others from the Banquet Feast, for they deny those who truly understand that the invitation to be part of God's community is by the gift of grace, not good works.

A point of clarification needs to be made: people with disabilities are not to be prized for their disability. As was cited previously, for many people with disabling conditions there is a profound sense of failure that they have been dealt by society. Coming into a gathering of Christians and being considered an honored guest is more than merely awkward. It challenges the very image of how the person with a disability sees him or herself. It is not unusual at all for the person with a disability in the context of a congregation or parish to struggle with their gifts that will arise in Christ's community.

To distribute this invitation, to make it known to others, will take a strategy, time, energy, persistence, and patience on behalf of congregations and parishes. Members of churches will need to be in touch with and be constantly present at regular functions of organizations and self-advocacy groups in their vicinity, like attending weekly or monthly meetings and political rallies of "People First" or the Association for Retarded Citizens (ARC), attending conferences like the Council for Exceptional Children (CEC), the Alliance for the Mentally Ill (AMI), or supporting a local l'Arche community or secular group home for people with disabilities. Some of these groups meet in church buildings but rarely is there a representative from the home church. Many group homes would welcome the informal support and caring contact. The act of reaching out of the Church and into the community of people with disabilities in the larger society will make a great impression on many public and private organizations.

Within the national offices and regional bodies of the Protestant churches and Roman Catholic churches are offices staffed by people who are knowledgeable about the resource materials that will enable congregations and parishes to be inclusive gatherings. Many of these staff people are waiting for churches to seek more information on this important issue. Information on the issues concerning people with disabilities should also be considered as part of seminary training. Currently there are some theological seminaries and divinity schools that offer courses just on ministry with people with disabilities, but these courses shouldn't be the only place where the concerns of people with disabilities are presented: They should be woven in all parts of theological education.

As was mentioned in Chapter 5, with the presence of people with disabilities in the midst of church life, often churches will become more knowledgeable of the needs and concerns of people with disabilities in general because it directly affects one member of the body of Christ. Invite people with disabilities to share their concerns during "Minutes for Mission," as well as in the sermons, seminars, and lecture series in the church and its denominational and seminary programs.

To extend an invitation to celebrate life: In conclusion, the celebration of the life of a person with a disabling condition, Christ's invited guest, is a moral act of the Christian community; it is "a cry of a people to covenant together."[288] It helps people to accept the sufferings of daily life, nourishing everyone and expressing to each other and the world around the Christian gathering that here is the living Christ's community in concrete and tangible ways. This is why Jesus, the servant, was sent by God, the Host, to "Go out into the roads and lanes, and compel people to come in, so that my house may be filled" (Luke 14:23). God's Banquet Feast of love awaits the eagerly awaited and anticipated presence of our company.

Notes

1. Brett Webb-Mitchell, "A Place for Persons with Disabilities of Mind and Body," *Religious Education* 81 (Fall 1986), 522–544.

2. Brett Webb-Mitchell, "The Place and Power of Acceptance in Pastoral Care with Persons Who Are Mentally Retarded," in *The Journal of Pastoral Care*, 1988, Vol. XLII, No. 4, pp. 351–362.

3. Jean Vanier, *Community and Growth (2nd Edition)* (Mahwah: Paulist Press, 1989).

4. Harold Wilke, *Creating the Caring Congregation* (Nashville, Abingdon Press, 1979), p. 30.

5. Parker Palmer, *The Active Life* (San Francisco: Harper Collins, 1990), p. 25.

6. Helen Featherstone, *There's A Difference in the Family* (New York, Penguin Press, 1981).

7. Ibid, p. 33.

8. Stanley Hauerwas, *Suffering Presence* (Notre Dame: University of Notre Dame Press, 1987).

9. Robert Scheerenberger, *A History of Mental Retardation* (Baltimore: Paul H. Brookes Publishing Company, 1983).

10. Ibid.

11. Jurgen Moltmann, *God in Creation* (New York, Harper and Row Publishing Company, 1985).

12. Ibid, p. 350.

13. Featherstone, *There's a Difference in the Family*.

14. Hauerwas, *Suffering Presence*.

15. Vanier, *Community and Growth*, pp. 95, 97.

16. The term "Kingdom of God" will be used in this book, referring to either the reign of God, or realm of God.

17. Thomas Groome, *Christian Religious Education* (San Francisco: Harper & Row, 1980).

18. Stanley Hauerwas, "The Gesture of a Truthful Story" in *Christian Existence Today* (Durham, NC: Labyrinth Press, 1988).

19. Michel Jeanneret, A Feast of Words (Chicago: University of Chicago, 1991).

20. In this book, I will address those individuals whom society has labeled as being 'disabled' as "people with a disabling condition," or "people with disabilities."

21. Erving Goffman, Stigma (New York: Simon and Schuster, 1963).

22. Susan Campling, Images of Ourselves (New York: Routledge and Kegan Paul, 1981).

23. Nicholas Hobbs, The Futures of Children (San Francisco: Jossey-Bass Publishing Company, 1981), p. 29.

24. Ibid.

25. Ibid, p. 1.

26. James J. Gallagher, "The Sacred and Profane Uses of Labeling," in Mental Retardation, 14 (1976).

27. Hobbs, Futures of Children, p. 11.

28. Joel Elizur and Salvador Minuchin, Institutionalizing Madness (New York: Basic Books, 1989), p. 24.

29. Gallagher, "Sacred And Profane Uses of Labeling."

30. Hobbs, Futures of Children.

31. J. Mercer "Psychological assessment and the rights of children" in Nicholas Hobbs Issues in the Classification of Children, Volume I (San Francisco: Jossey-Bass Publishing Company, 1975).

See also Diana v. State Board of Education, Civil Action No. C70 37 RFP(N.D. Cal. January 7, 1970, and June 18, 1973).

32. James Carrier, Learning Disability (Westport: Greenwood Press, 1986).

33. Scheerenberger, History of Mental Retardation.

34. Hobbs, Futures of Children, p. 30.

35. Steven Jay Gould, The Mismeasure of Man (New York, W. W. Norton Publishing Company, 1981), p. 155.

36. Erica Goode, "Sick, or just quirky?" U. S. News & World Report, February 10, 1992, pp. 49, 50.

37. Jules Henry, Pathways to Madness (New York: Vintage Book Press, 1973).

38. Jean-Marc-Gaspard Itard, The Wild Boy of Aveyron (Englewood Cliffs: Prentice Hall Publishing Company, 1962).

39. "AAMR Board Approves New MR Definition," AAMR News & Notes, 5 (July/August 1992), p. 1.

40. Samuel Kirk and J. J. Gallagher, Educating Exceptional Children, Sixth Edition (Boston: Houghton-Mifflin Publishing Company, 1989).

41. Lynn Feagans, "Learning Disabilities And Emotional/Behavioral Problems," in Betty Epanchin and Jim Paul's Emotional Problems Of Childhood And Adolescence (Columbus, OH: Merrill Publishing Company, 1987).

42. Comprehensive Assessment and Service (CASE) Information System (Washington DC: American Speech-Language-Hearing Association, 1976).

43. Kirk and Gallagher, Educating Exceptional Children.

44. R. Frisina, "Report of the Committee to Redefine Deaf and Hard Of Hearing For Educational Purposes" (1974).

45. Henry Kisor, What's That Pig Outdoors? (New York: Hill and Wang Publishing Company, 1990), p. 255.

46. Kirk and Gallagher, *Educating Exceptional Children*, p. 328.

47. Oliver Sacks, *Seeing Voices* (Berkeley: University of California Press, 1989).

48. Kisor, *What's That Pig Outdoors?*

49. N. Barraga, *Visual Handicaps and Learning (Rev. Ed.)* (Austin: Exceptional Resources, 1983).

50. Kirk and Gallagher, *Educating Exceptional Children*, p. 349.

51. Ibid.

52. Ibid.

53. Ibid.

54. U.S. Office of Education. "Definition of Severely Handicapped Children." *Code of Federal Regulations* (Title 45, Section 121.2). Washington, DC: Bureau of Education for the Handicapped.

55. Michael Dorris, *The Broken Cord* (New York: Houghton-Mifflin, 1989).

56. Don Bailey and Rune Simeonsson, "Critical Issues Underlying Research and Intervention with Families of Young Handicapped Children," *Journal of the Division For Early Childhood*, Vol, 9, pp. 38–48, 1984.

57. Kirk and Gallagher, *Educating Exceptional Children*, p. 460.

58. Ibid.

59. Stanley Hauerwas and William Willimon, *Resident Aliens* (Nashville, TN: Abingdon Press, 1989).

60. Kisor, *What's That Pig Outdoors?*, p. 7.

61. Vanier, *Community and Growth.*

62. Stanley Hauerwas, "The Church and the Mentally Handicapped: A Continuing Challenge to Our Imaginations" in *Dispatches from the Front* (Durham: Duke University Press, NYP).

63. Margaret Visser, *The Rituals of Dinner* (New York: Penguin Books, 1991), p. 86.

64. See B.F. Skinner, *Beyond Freedom and Dignity* (New York: Alfred Knopf Incorporated, 1971); and James Carrier, *Learning Disability* (Westport: Greenwood Press, 1986).

65. Scheerenberger, *History of Mental Retardation*, p. 3.

66. Ibid, p. 4.

67. Ibid, p. 7.

68. Ibid, p. 8.

69. Leo Kanner, *History Of The Care And Study Of The Mentally Retarded* (Springfield: Charles C. Thomas Pub., 1964).

D. MacMillan, *Mental Retardation In School And Society* (Boston: Little, Brown, & Co., 1977).

70. Burton Cooper, "The Disabled God" *Theology Today* 49 (July 1992), p. 174.

71. Ibid, p. 174.

72. Walter Brueggemann, *Interpretation Commentary: Genesis* (Louisville, KY: John Knox/Westminster Press, 1982), p. 30.

73. Ibid, p. 27.

74. Ibid, pp. 48–54.

75. D. Silverman, "The Jewish View of Education for the Handicapped," *Your Child* (New York: United Synagogue Commission on Jewish Education, 1967), p. 17.

76. Dorothee Soelle, *Suffering* (Philadelphia: Fortress Press, 1975), p. 166.

77. Paul Tillich, *The Shaking of The Foundations* (New York: Scribners and Sons, 1948), p. 162.

78. Ellen Nelson, "The Local Church As A Resource For Persons With Mental Retardation Living In The Community: A Study of the Emerging Roles and Service Patterns." Unpublished Manuscript. Ph.D. Dissertation, Brandeis University, 1983, pp. 21, 22.

79. H. Sigerist, "The Special Position of the Sick" in C. Landy, *Culture, Disease and Healing* (New York: Macmillan Publishing Company, 1977), p. 391.

80. Ibid, p. 392.

81. Kanner, *History of Care and Study of Mentally Retarded.*

82. Scheerenberger, *History of Mental Retardation*, p. 34.

83. Nelson, "Local Church as Resource," p. 24.

84. Ibid.

85. Kanner, *History of Care and Study of Mentally Retarded*, p. 3.

86. Nelson, "Local Church as Resource," p. 25.

87. Frank Cross (Editor), *The Oxford Dictionary of The Christian Church* (New York: Oxford University Press, 1978), p. 1170.

88. Peter Brown, *The Book of Kells* (London: Thames and Hudson, 1980).

89. Howard Gardner, *Art Through The Ages, 6th Edition* (New York: Harcourt, Brace, Jovanovich, Inc., 1970), pp. 559–560.

90. Scheerenberger, *History of Mental Retardation*, p. 34.

91. Ibid, p. 34.

92. Ibid, p. 33.

93. James Burke, *The Day the Universe Changed* (Boston: Little, Brown, and Company, 1985), p. 112.

94. Paul Tillich, *The Courage To Be* (New Haven: Yale University Press, 1952), p. 58.

95. MacMillan, *Mental Retardation In School And Society*, p. 11.

96. Cross, *Oxford Dictionary Of The Christian Church*, p. 849.

97. Nelson, "Local Church as Resource," p. 27.

98. Kanner, *History of Care and Study of Mentally Retarded*, p. 7.

99. Martin Luther, *Colloquia Mensalia* (London: William DuGard, 1652).

100. Scheerenberger, *History of Mental Retardation*, p. 32.

101. John McNeil, *Calvin's Institutes of the Christian Religion, Vol. I* (Philadelphia: Westminster Press, 1960).

102. Ibid, pp. 200, 507.

103. Ibid, p. 153.

104. Elizur and Minuchin, *Institutionalizing Madness*, p. 3.

105. Sigerist, "The Special Position of the Sick," p. 392.

106. Scheerenberger, *History of Mental Retardation*, p. 47.

107. M. J. McCulloch, "Animal Facilitated Therapy: Overview and Future Direction," *National Forum*, Vol. 46, No. 1, 1986, p. 19.

108. Scheerenberger, *History of Mental Retardation*, pp. 35–36.

109. MacMillan, *Mental Retardation in School and Society.*

110. Kanner, *History of Care and Study of Mentally Retarded.*

111. Roy Porter, *A Social History of Madness* (New York: Dutton Publishing Company, 1989), p. 15.

112. Scheerenberger, *History of Mental Retardation*, p. 92.

113. Ibid, p. 92.

114. Ibid, p. 94.

115. Stanley Vitello and Ronald Soskin, *Mental Retardation: Its Social and Legal Context* (Englewood Cliffs: Prentice Hall Publishing Company, 1985), p. 24.

116. Ibid, p. 25.

117. Itard, *Wild Boy*. Also see Scheerenberger, *History of Mental Retardation*, pp. 74–78.

118. Scheerenberger, *History of Mental Retardation*, p. 78.

119. Vitello and Soskin, *Mental Retardation: Context*, pp. 26–27.

120. Oliver Sacks, "Forsaking the Mentally Ill" in *The New York Times*, Feb. 13, 1991.

121. Douglas John Hall, *God and Human Suffering: An Exercise in the Theology of the Cross* (Minneapolis: Augsburg Publishing House, 1986), p. 97.

122. John Westerhoff and Brett Webb-Mitchell, "Liturgy: Integrating People with Mental Retardation Into the Life of Religious Communities." Unpublished essay.

123. Stanley Hauerwas, *Naming the Silences* (Grand Rapids, MI: Wm. Eerdmans Publishing Company, 1990), p. 40.

124. Ibid, p. 48.

125. Ibid, p. 41.

126. Ibid, p. 49.

127. Kenneth Surin, *Theology and the Problem of Evil* (Oxford, UK: Basil Blackwell, 1986), p. 27.

128. Hauerwas, *Naming the Silences*, p. 52.

129. Ibid, pp. 53, 58.

130. Hauerwas, "Church and Mentally Handicapped," p. 10.

131. Vanier, *Community and Growth*, p. 161.

132. Visser, *Rituals of Dinner*, p. ix.

133. Brett Webb-Mitchell, "L'Arche: An Ethnographic Study of Persons with Disabilities Living In Community With Non-Disabled People." Unpublished doctoral dissertation, University of North Carolina-Chapel Hill, December, 1988.

134. Vanier, *Community and Growth*, p. 322.

135. Ibid, p. 314.

136. Hauerwas, "Church and Mentally Handicapped."

137. Vanier, *Community and Growth*, p. 47.

138. Richard Katz, "Empowerment And Synergy: Expanding The Community's Healing Resources." Unpublished manuscript, Cambridge, MA: Harvard University, 1984, p. 1.

139. National Organization on Disability, *That All May Worship* (Washington, DC: National Organization on Disability, 1992), p. 50.

140. Sallie McFague, *Speaking in Parables* (Philadelphia: Fortress Press, 1975), p. 1.

141. Borg, *Jesus: A New Vision* (New York: Harper and Row, 1987), p. 198.

142. Lesslie Newbigin, *Sign Of The Kingdom* (Grand Rapids, MI: Wm. Eerdmans Press, 1980).

143. Borg, *Jesus: New Vision*, p. 199.

144. Wendell Berry, *What Are People For?* (San Francisco: North Point Press, 1990), p. 200.

145. Newbigin, *Sign of the Kingdom*, p. 69.

146. Joseph Fitzmyer, *The Gospel According to Luke, X-XXIV*, Anchor Bible Commentary (New York: Doubleday, 1985), p. 1041.

147. Carroll Stuhlmueller, "The Gospel According To St. Luke" in *The Jerome Biblical Commentary* (Englewood Cliffs: Prentice-Hall, 1968), p. 147.

148. Joseph Fitzmyer writes that "dropsy" is a result of edema, an "abnormal accumulation of serous fluids in connective tissues or cavities of the body accompanied by swelling, distention, or defective circulation." See Fitzmyer, *The Gospel According To Luke X-XXIV, Anchor Bible Commentary*, p. 1041.

149. Fitzmyer, *Gospel According to Luke*, p. 1041.

150. Stuhlmueller, C.P. "The Gospel According To St. Luke."

151. Fitzmyer, *Gospel According to Luke*, p. 1048.

152. S. Maclean Gilmour, *Interpreter's Bible Commentary: Luke And John* (Nashville, TN: Abingdon Press, 1982), p. 258.

153. Visser, *Rituals of Dinner*, pp. 27–29.

154. Jeanneret, *Feast of Words*, p. 13.

155. William Barclay, *The Gospel Of Luke* (Philadelphia: Westminster Press, 1975).

156. Jeanneret, *Feast of Words*, p. 37.

157. Fitzmyer, *Gospel According to Luke*, p. 1049.

158. See Fitzmyer, Stuhlmueller, and Barclay.

159. Visser, *Rituals of Dinner*, p. 100.

160. Ibid, p. 101.

161. *Interpreter's Bible Commentary*, p. 258.

162. Stuhlmueller, *The Jerome Biblical Commentary*, p. 147.

163. Fitzmyer, *Gospel According to Luke*, p. 1057.

164. Ibid, p. 1054.

165. Frederick Buechner, *Wishful Thinking* (New York: Harper & Row, 1973), p. 67.

166. Whitney Chadwick, *Women, Art, And Society* (New York: Thames And Hudson, 1990), p. 346.
Wendy Slatkin, *Women Artists In History, 2nd Edition* (Englewood Cliffs: Prentice-Hall, 1990), p. 187.

167. Stanley Hauerwas, *A Community of Character* (Notre Dame: University of Notre Dame Press, 1981), pp. 60–69.

168. Ibid, p. 60.

169. Fitzmyer, *Gospel According to Luke*, p. 1054.

170. Brueggemann, *Interpretation Commentary: Genesis*, pp. 16–22.

171. Berry, *What Are People For?*, p. 200.

172. Wolfhart Pannenberg, *Theology And The Kingdom Of God* (Philadelphia: Westminster Press, 1977), p. 93.

173. Katz, "Empowerment and Synergy," p. 29.

174. Berry, *What Are People For?*, p. 201.

175. Vanier, *Community and Growth*, pp. 55, 56.

176. Tracey Warren, "Disabilities Concerns Week Helps to Raise Awareness of the Physically Challenged," in *Whitworthian*, Vol. 81, No. 16, 1991.

177. Annie Dillard, *Holy The Firm* (New York: Harper & Row, Publishing Company, 1977), p. 59.

178. Ibid, p. 59.

179. Brett Webb-Mitchell, "The Prophetic Voice of Parents," *New Oxford Review*, in process of being published.

180. Thomas Groome, *Christian Religious Education* (New York: Harper & Row Publishing Company, 1980).

181. Vanier, *Community And Growth*, p. 169.

182. Lambros Kamperidis, "Philoxenia and Hospitality" in *Parabola*, 15 (Winter 1990), p. 5.

183. Hauerwas, *A Peaceable Kingdom*, p. 91.

184. Helen Luke, "The Stranger Within" in *Parabola*, 15 (Winter 1990), pp. 17–19.

185. Kamperidis, "Philoxenia and Hospitality," p. 5.

186. An interview with John Callahan, Portland, Oregon, March, 1991.

187. Paul Theroux, "An Edwardian On The Concorde: Graham Greene As I Knew Him" in *New York Times Book Review*, April 21, 1991.

188. Marie Balter and Richard Katz, *Nobody's Child* (New York: Addison Wesley, 1991).

189. This situational game was taught to me by Andre Branch at Whitworth College when he was there as the Director of Multicultural Affairs.

190. Wilke, *Creating The Caring Congregation*.

191. Oliver Sacks, *The Man Who Mistook His Wife For A Hat* (New York: Harper & Row, Publishing Company, 1987), p. 174.

192. Pamela Wickham-Searl, "Mothers with a Mission," in Philip Ferguson, Dianne Ferguson, and Steven Taylor (Eds.) *Interpreting Disability: A Qualitative Reader* (New York: Teachers College Press), pp. 251–274.

193. Hauerwas, "Church and Mentally Handicapped."

194. A fuller explanation of this pedagogical theory is in the following article: Brett Webb-Mitchell, "Listen and Learn from Narratives That Tell a Story," in *Religious Education*, 85, 4, 1991, pp. 615–630.

195. Alisdair MacIntyre, *After Virtue* (Notre Dame, IN: University of Notre Dame Press, 1984), p. 106.

196. Ibid, p. 105.

197. Vanier, *Community and Growth*, p. 47.

198. Ibid, p. 161.

199. Brett Webb-Mitchell, *God Plays Piano, Too: The Spiritual Lives of Disabled Children* (New York: Crossroad Publishing Company, 1993), pp. 130–131.

200. Lavinia Derwent, *Joseph and the Coat of Many Colors* (New York: Scholastic Book Services, 1965).

201. Brett Webb-Mitchell, "Some Lessons From the Spiritual Narratives of Children with Disabilities," presented at APRRE, Indianapolis, Indiana, Nov. 5–7, 1992.

202. Vivian Gussin Paley, *The Boy Who Would Be a Helicopter* (Cambridge, MA: Harvard University, 1990), p. xii.

203. Kirk and Gallagher, *Educating Exceptional Children*, p. 41.

204. Hauerwas, "Church and Mentally Handicapped."

205. Kirk and Gallagher, *Educating Exceptional Children*, p. 41.

See also Patricia Porter and Grace Lane, "Programming to Meet the Needs of Handicapped Children: Curriculum and Environmental Adaptations" in Jim Paul, Editor, *The Exceptional Child* (Syracuse, NY: Syracuse University Press, 1983).

206. Kirk and Gallagher, *Educating Exceptional Children*.

207. Balter and Katz, *Nobody's Child*, p. xiii.

208. Porter & Lane, "Programming to Meet Needs of Handicapped Children," p. 91.

209. Visser, *Rituals of Dinner*, p. ix.

210. Vanier, *Community and Growth*, p. 42.

211. Parker Palmer, *To Know as We Are Known* (San Francisco: Harper & Row, 1984).

212. In Hebrew the word is "tselem" meaning likeness, or resemblance, of God's making human beings in his own image.

213. Brueggemann, *Interpretation Commentary: Genesis*.

In using the term, "create," I use it in the meaning of "to craft," not creation out of nothing. To create or craft in this sense is to take that which already exists and shape it into what the craftsperson wants to create.

214. Maxine Greene, "What Happened to Imagination?" in Kieran Egan and Dan Nadaner, *Imagination as Education* (New York: Teachers College Press, 1989).

215. Edward Robinson, *The Language of Mystery* (London: SCM Press, 1987).

216. Visser, *Rituals of Dinner*, p. 137.

217. Ibid, p. 138.

218. See Elliot Eisner, *National Forum*, and Elliot Eisner, *The Educational Imagination, 2nd Edition* (New York: Macmillan Press, 1985).

219. Visser, *Rituals of Dinner*, p. 23.

220. Victor Turner, *The Ritual Process* (Ithaca, NY: Cornell University, 1977).

221. Westerhoff and Webb-Mitchell, "Liturgy: Integrating People."

222. Elizer Shore, "The Soul of the Community" *Parabola* (Spring 1992), p. 18.

223. Jeanneret, *Feast of Words*, p. 28.

224. Visser, *Rituals of Dinner*, p. 27.

225. Stanley Hauerwas, "Church and Mentally Handicapped."

226. Ibid.

227. Ibid.

228. Ibid.

229. Jeanneret, *Feast of Words*, p. 112.

230. Ibid, p. 113.

231. Ibid, p. 177.

232. Barry Lopez, *Winter Count* (New York: Charles Scribners' Sons, 1981), p. 62.

233. Jim McLaughlin, a good friend, shared these thoughts with me on one of my many moves in life.

234. Visser, *Rituals of Dinner*, p. 101.

235. Ibid, p. 94.

236. A figure-ground reversal of sorts.

237. Denis Huere, "Room For The Dance" in *Parabola* 40 (Winter 1990), p. 36.

238. Visser, *Rituals of Dinner*, pp. 1, 2.

239. Westerhoff and Webb-Mitchell, "Liturgy: Integrating People."

240. Hauerwas, "The Gesture of a Truthful Story."

241. Robinson, *The Language of Mystery*.
Mary Warnock, *Imagination* (Berkeley: University of California Press, 1978).

242. Webb-Mitchell, *God Plays Piano, Too*, p. 123.

243. Anthony Giddens, *Sociology, 2nd Edition* (Orlando, FL: Harcourt Brace Jovanovich, Inc., 1987), p. 11.

244. D. Stephen Long, *Living the Discipline* (Grand Rapids, MI: Wm. B. Eerdmans Publishing Company, 1992), pp. 9, 10.

245. *Mirriam Webster's Collegiate Dictionary, 10th Edition* (Springfield, MA: 1993), p. 489.

246. Keith Thomas in Jan Bremmer and Herman Roodenburg, *A Cultural History of Gesture* (Ithaca, NY: Cornell University Press, 1991), p. 1.

247. Anthony Cohen, *The Symbolic Construction of Community* (London, UK: Tavistock, 1985), p. 15.

248. Clifford Geertz, *Interpretation of Cultures* (New York: Basic Books, 1973), p. 6.

249. Thomas in *A Cultural History of Gesture*, p. 6.

250. Walter Ong, *Presence of the Word* (Minneapolis: University of Minnesota Press, 1986), p. 147.

251. Peter and Jill de Villiers, *Early Language* (Cambridge, MA: Harvard University Press, 1979), p. 4.

252. Sacks, *Seeing Voices*, p. 120.

253. Karl Barth, *Commentary on Romans* (New York: Oxford University Press, 1968), p. 502.

254. John McNeill, *Calvin's Institutes*, p. 1281.

255. Ibid., p. 1281.

256. Hauerwas, "The Gesture of a Truthful Story," p. 106.

257. Ibid, p. 106.

258. Jerome Bruner, *Toward a Theory of Instruction* (Cambridge, MA: Harvard University Press, 1966), p. 151.

259. Ibid., p. 151.

260. World Council of Churches, *Baptism, Eucharist and Ministry* (Geneva, Switzerland: World Council of Churches Press, 1982).

261. Webb-Mitchell, "Place and Power of Acceptance," p. 359.

262. Sacks, *Man Who Mistook His Wife*, p. 80.

263. Ibid., p. 83.

264. Judith Martin, "We Can't Get along without Manners," in *News and Observer*, Sunday, Feb. 13, 1994, p. 2E.

265. Visser, *Rituals of Dinner*, p. 3.

266. Ibid., p. 3.

267. Hauerwas, "Church and Mentally Handicapped."

268. Jeanneret, *Feast of Words*.

269. Paul Jordan-Smith, "And The Word Was Made Flesh," *Parabola*, 17 (Fall 1992), p. 85.

270. Ibid, p. 87.

271. Visser, *Rituals of Dinner*, p. 36.

272. Jordan-Smith, "Word Made Flesh," p. 85.

273. Geoffrey Wainwright, *Doxology* (New York: Oxford University Press, 1984), p. 41.

274. Ibid, p. 41.

275. Visser, *Rituals of Dinner*, p. 37.

276. Wainwright, *Doxology*, pp. 318, 343.

277. Vanier, *Community and Growth*, p. 165.

278. Frederick Buechner, *Wishful Thinking* (New York: Harper & Row Publishers, 1979), p. 6.

279. Wainwright, *Doxology*, p. 418.

280. In the history of the Church, this verse has also been interpreted in a violent fashion, like during the Spanish Inquisition, when people were killed if they didn't come to church and convert to Christianity.

281. I take this idea from the book by Vivian Gussin Paley, *You Can't Say You Can't Play* (Cambridge, MA: Harvard University Press, 1992).

282. Hauerwas, "The Church and the Mentally Handicapped: A Continuing Challenge to Our Imaginations," p. 11.

283. Vanier, *Community and Growth*, p. 69.

284. Hauerwas, "Church and Mentally Handicapped."

285. John Dominic Crossan, *The Historical Life of Jesus* (New York: Harper Collins, 1991), p. 262.

286. Ibid., pp. 263, 264.

287. Vanier, *Community and Growth*, p. 41.

288. Ibid., p. 314.